Practical Upholstery

W9-BGZ-230

Practical Upholstery

C. Howes F.A.M.U.

A Drake Publication
Sterling Publishing Co., Inc.   New York

Published in 1980 by
Sterling Publishing Co., Inc.
Two Park Avenue
New York, N.Y. 10016

© Evans Brothers Ltd. 1973
First published in 1950 as Practical Upholstery.
Published by arrangement with Evans Brothers Ltd.
This edition available in the United States and
the Philippine Islands only.

ISBN 0-8069-8578-X
Previously
ISBN 0-273-44536-0

Contents

Chapter one	History, Traditions, Prospects	7
Chapter two	Tools, Needles, Workshop Requirements	9
Chapter three	Materials	13
Chapter four	Springs and Springing	20
Chapter five	Frames	27
Chapter six	General Principles and Useful Hints	32
Chapter seven	Planning and Cutting Covers	36
Chapter eight	Hides and Moroccos	41
Chapter nine	Loose Seats and Other Small Seats	45
Chapter ten	Stools, Slipper Box	50
Chapter eleven	The Fireside Easy	56
Chapter twelve	Open Arm Fireside Chair	60
Chapter thirteen	Fireside Chair	63
Chapter fourteen	T.V., Sewing or Knitting Chair	67
Chapter fifteen	A New Form of Comfort	72
Chapter sixteen	Period Wing Armchair	75
Chapter seventeen	Three-Piece Suite	78
Chapter eighteen	Contemporary Three-Piece Suite	93
Chapter nineteen	A Well-Cushioned Suite	101
Chapter twenty	Box Ottoman	105
Chapter twenty-one	Divan Bed	109
Chapter twenty-two	Deep Buttoned Headboard	113
Chapter twenty-three	Deep Buttoning	116
Chapter twenty-four	Running Repairs	119
Index		126

Introduction

One of the nicknames bestowed on the upholsterer by other sections of the furniture trade is *Ragtacker*. I have been engaged in the ragtacking business for a number of years and have tacked rags, or, to be more polite, fabrics on quite a varied selection of articles ranging from kiddies' chairs to motor gun-boats over 100ft. long.

The chief object of the upholsterer's craft, however, is to provide pieces of furniture comfortable to sit on and pleasant to look upon. It takes time and patience to achieve this object. Methods and designs are constantly changing and the good craftsman is always learning. During my early days at the bench I found it difficult to acquire sound knowledge and there were few books dealing with the subject. I hope, therefore, that this volume will help both those in the trade and home craftsmen to gain an insight into the craft.

Of course, as in all the old handicraft trades, machinery and pre-fabrication are playing their part. This is modern industrial progress which has its counterpart in almost every trade and profession. Some of the materials and components that are readily at hand in a factory or work-shop are not always available to the worker at home. Consequently alternative suggestions and methods are given.

I trust that all who are interested in the craft of upholstery will find some assistance in this book, and become worthy modern successors of the old-time craftsmen who took pride in turning out first-class work.

The drawings were contributed by my brother S. C. Howes and Mr. C. H. Hayward to whom I am greatly indebted, and I offer my grateful thanks. I also wish to acknowledge the kind assistance given by firms in lending photographs of high grade upholstery showing workmanship that is worthy of the best traditions of the trade.

C. Howes

Chapter one

History, Tradition, Prospects

Egyptian limestone statuette c2600BC
British Museum

When one considers the tremendous technological developments that are taking place today it seems somewhat trivial to be writing about ways of upholstering furniture. Upon further reflection, however, one realises this is the age of more leisure for more people than any previous period, and with it comes the need for comfortable resting accommodation. Even the spacemen require upholstery to lie upon. Air travel firms pride themselves on the comfort of their seating; office workers sit-out their working hours on upholstered seats instead of the hard wooden stools; and the same story can be told of many other branches of industry and leisure.

The origin of the chair goes back a very long time, probably about 5,000 years. Much of the knowledge of the early chairs and stools has been gained through the Egyptians' belief in the life hereafter. When their rulers and prominent people died many of their personal belongings were placed in the tombs with them. Paintings, carvings on stone and remains of wooden furniture show that the Egyptian cabinet-makers knew how to make good mortise-and-tenon joints and dowel joints 2,000 or more years B.C. The upholsterer had not specialised quite so early but chairs, stools, and beds had webbing of hide straps interlaced across them. Linen cushions were also used, and one carving on stone dated around 2,800 B.C. shows a cushion hung over the back of a chair. The way it is draped is very similar to the current vogue of draping polyether foam cushions over the arms of easy chairs. Not only the Egyptians but other Middle East people, the Greek and Byzantine Empires also, and eventually the Chinese enjoyed the use of chairs several thousand years ago.

The tent-makers of the early days with their drapes and hangings were probably the forerunners of the upholsterers. One of the worthy members of this ancient trade was that great traveller and apostle, St Paul. Among the oldest of the City of London Guilds is the Worshipful Company of Upholders. It was granted a coat of arms consisting of a shield with three tents emblazoned in 1465. This coat of arms is carved on one of the columns in St Paul's Cathedral. According to the City records the earliest mention of its members is 1258.

Many kind words have been spoken about *craftsmanship* but I'm afraid it is little more than

'lip service' when it is craft versus hard cash, especially in the present day economic set-up. However, for a lad entering this trade the future is probably as good as in most trades. At least he will still have to use his hands as well as his brain and should get some satisfaction out of creating a useful and pleasing end product. Also as he learns more of the trade he will find there are quite interesting jobs to be obtained, including work on yachts and motor cruisers, many of which need interior trimming, carpet fitting and upholstery. In addition liners, aircraft, and hotels all get hard wear on their furnishings and either new items or repairs are needed.

As the prosperity of a person improves the desire to express individuality in the home usually increases. So long as this part of the human character remains, the 'bespoke' or 'custom built' section of the trade will flourish and craftsmen will be needed to produce upholstery that has character and comfort.

Left: Seated Egyptian figure c2600BC
British Museum

Below: Seating in the first class of a BOAC 747

Chapter two

Tools, Needles, Workshop Requirements, Machinery

One of the minor blessings of the upholsterer's craft is that it does not require a large number of expensive tools. A quite modest outlay will buy everything required.

Most trades require tools for measuring, and upholstery is no exception. A ·6m. (two-foot) boxwood rule and a 1·5m. (five-foot) linen tape are both necessary, and a flexible spring steel tape is often found useful. These can be bought cheaply, but it is advisable to consider quality before price whenever purchasing tools.

Hammers The upholsterer's hammer was once his most important and most used tool. Tacks were then considered the chief method of attaching covers to a wooden frame, but in many factories and workshops the stapling gun and staples have almost taken over completely. These will be dealt with later. Meanwhile, to return to the hammer which will still be needed for many bespoke jobs, there are two main types; the tack hammer and the cabriole hammer. The shape of both is similar but the cabriole has a much smaller head—approx. 6·25mm. ($\frac{1}{4}$in.) diameter—and was extensively used when show-wood furniture was fashionable. They are shown in Fig. 1. Before the staples took over the magnetic hammer was much in demand. Tacks were picked out from the upholsterer's mouth, where they were usually carried, by the magnetised head of the hammer and driven directly into the frames or item being covered.

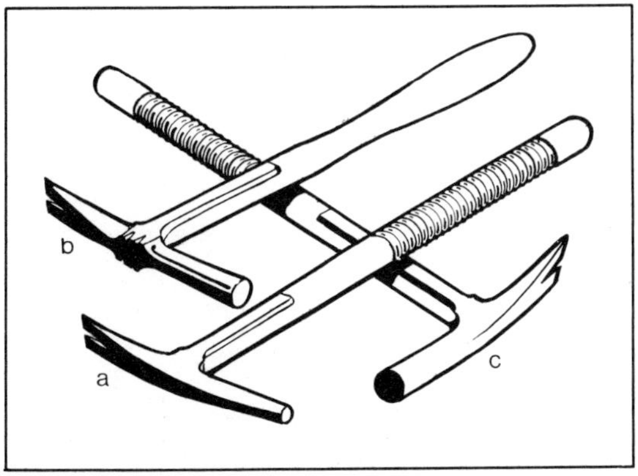

Fig. 1 Types of hammers used in upholstery: **A** shows the cabriole hammer with small head. Both **A** and **C** have 'ringed' handles, whilst **B** has a pear-shaped handle.

Fig. 2 Strong scissors, fairly heavy without being cumbersome.

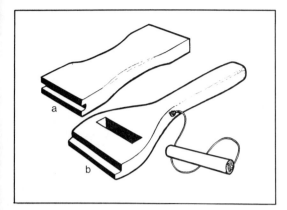

Fig. 3 Alternative forms of web strainers.
A shows the plain hardwood kind in which the groove fits over the edge of the framework with the webbing beneath. **B** is the bat type. The looped web is inserted in the slot and the peg inserted in the loop.

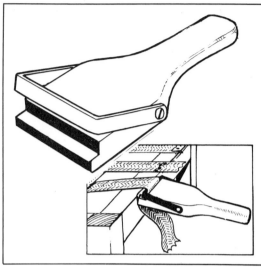

Fig. 4 Lever-type strainer with rebated end. The inset drawing shows how the web passes through the lever and beneath the end.

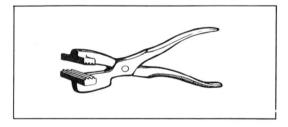

Fig. 5 Web pincers with corrugated jaws. These can be used for short ends, though long lengths can be gripped if the web is looped. In the case of polished wood the webbing should be passed beneath the projecting lower jaw so that the metal does not damage the wood.

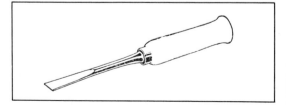

Fig. 6 Upholsterer's ripping chisel. Used to remove the tacks when upholstering.

Cutting Tools A good pair of scissors, Fig. 2, measuring about 250mm. (10in.) overall, fairly heavy but not cumbersome, is a necessity. A reputable maker's name stamped on should ensure their keeping a good edge when they need re-sharpening. Also required for trimming off, especially P.V.C. fabrics, hide etc., is a sharp pointed knife. The type does not matter much so long as it has a sharp edge and point and can be re-sharpened quickly and often when in use.

Web Strainers Once much in demand when the base of most upholstery was built up from a webbed base. Not so much used now, but still needed for various items. Several types are used, the simplest being just a plain piece of hardwood, shaped as shown in Fig. 3A, with a groove at one end. The web is brought over the plain top and under the grooved bottom end, as the strainer is held on the edge of the frame being webbed. It is gripped with the left hand and levered down until the strain is sufficient. A similar type has four or five spikes at one end, instead of being plain, but this is not much in favour as it is liable to damage the web.

Another design is shown in Fig. 3B. With this type the web is folded and passed through the opening and the bar is inserted in the loop. The bottom end of the strainer is placed on the frame and levered over until tight enough. Many upholsterers prefer the lever-type strainers. The loose end of the webbing is passed through the lever, and allowed to hang over the edge of the chair rail. The rebated foot of the strainer is placed upon the webbing and the handle levered over, so pulling the webbing taut as in Fig. 4. Another straining tool is the web pincers, Fig. 5, more often called web nippers. These have corrugated jaws and are used on short ends of web, but they often prove handy for pulling other materials tight.

The tools described above are all used in the making of upholstery, but the ripping chisel, Fig. 6, and mallet are for the unmaking. That is, on repair work they are needed to remove the tacks from the frame. The ripping chisel is held against the head of the tack and given a sharp blow with the mallet, thus forcing the tack from the wood. This should be done in the direction of the grain of the wood.

A medium, half-round rasp for rasping around facings, or where an edge is about to be tacked, is also required. Add a screw-driver or two, a pair of pliers, a pair of pincers, a medium-sized joiner's hammer, and a bradawl to complete the average upholsterer's kit with the exception of needles.

Needles Once again the changing needs of the trade does not require the constant use of the various types of needles but they are still needed for many repair jobs. See Fig. 7. The ordinary mattress needle is made in various sizes up to 400mm. (16in.) long and is double-pointed with an eye at one end. A 225mm. (9in.) or 250mm. (10in.) and a 350mm. (14in.) will be found to be the most useful. This needle is circular in section throughout its length, but its near relation, the bayonet or spear-pointed needle, is triangular for approximately a third of its length.

A most useful member of the family is the half-circular needle, which is also made in a number of sizes. These are used in places where it is difficult or impossible to work with a straight needle.

Last comes the spring needle, which, as its name implies, is used mainly for sewing the springs to the webs and the hessian. There are a number of jobs, however, where it is very useful, places where a straight needle is awkward and a circular one is

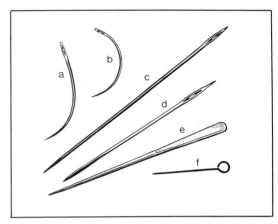

Fig. 7 Needles, regulators and skewers. **A** Spring needle; used for sewing springs to webs and hessians etc.: **B** Half-circular needle; used for sewing scrim and covers at awkward places: **C** Mattress or straight double-pointed needle; for running-through the first stuffing: **D** Bayonet or spear-pointed needle; for stitching rolls or edges: **E** Regulator; used to regulate the stuffing: **F** Upholsterer's skewer; used for temporarily holding hessian, scrim, cover and similar materials in place.

not stout enough. Upholsterer's skewers from 75–100mm. (3 to 4in.) in length are used to hold scrim, and coverings, etc., temporarily in position.

With the increasing use of Latex and Polyether foam, rubberised hair, fibre pads, lintafelt etc., the use of needles is now limited, although on repair work and hand-sprung jobs they are still needed. Skewers 87·5mm. (3½in.) or 100mm. (4in.) are still very useful, also the regulator, Fig. 7E, much used to regulate stuffing and especially when stitching rolls and edges. 250mm. (10in.) is a useful size.

The main workshop necessities are a pair of stout trestles, and a board on trestles or a table for cutting out materials. The trestles require wooden fillets all round the tops to keep the work in hand from slipping off, as in Fig. 8. A bag made of canvas or stout mattress ticking with about four compartments is needed for the various sizes of tacks. Add a white apron with a large pocket in front and you have the average upholsterer's working outfit.

Fig. 8 Trestles on which chair frames are stood They are about ·75m. (2ft. 6in.) high by ·9m. (3ft.) long. The wood fillets around the top prevent work from falling off. They are sometimes padded.

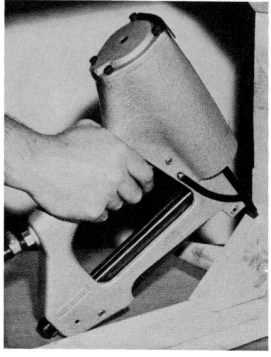

Fig. 9 Pneumatic stapler in use.

The homeworker will not require many mechanical aids other than a good sewing machine with a piping foot attached.

For the trade generally many mechanized and power tools and machines are becoming available, including power sewing machines working at high speeds with many devices for piping and ruching and for closing cushion openings. Carding machines are not required so much now where fibre pads, foam sheet, and lintafelt have ousted traditional materials, but are still needed in repair shops. Electric cutting machines are used in factories, and electric shears are available. Cushion-making machines for making spring interior cushions are less in use now with latex and polyether foam taking the place of spring cushions. Loose seat presses are used to hold the linters and cover in place whilst it is tacked or stapled round.

Recently a number of stapling machines have come onto the market, see Fig. 9. At first the machines were filled with staples which were forced out by a trigger action. Compressed air systems have come to the fore on the larger units, and portable guns, electrically operated, are also available.

Air tools must be properly serviced, maintaining the correct air pressure and be well lubricated. All these tools are essentially for the larger workshops and factories. For the homeworker making single items the hand tools are sufficient.

Chapter three

Materials

With the big changes brought about by the use of foams, many of the older materials and stuffings used in upholstery have taken a back seat. At the same time if a full knowledge of the trade is desired it is as well to have a working knowledge of the traditional methods and materials used.

Webbing Beginning at the bottom, webbing was the base of most upholstery. It was, and still is, made in a number of grades, the highest being a black and white twill weave of pure flax. Various other qualities of black and white web are made of mixtures of jute and cotton, or hemp, whilst sometimes linen threads are woven into the selvedges. It is generally 50mm. (2in.) wide, but can be obtained 53mm. (2⅛in.) and 56mm. (2¼in.) wide in certain qualities. Webbing made of polypropylene is a recent addition.

Plain brown or striped brown webbings are a cheaper grade, mainly all jute and of a plain weave. A large amount of it is produced in India and is obtainable in widths varying from 37·5mm. (1½in.) to 75mm. (3in.).

Springs and springing play such an important part in upholstery that they are dealt with in a separate chapter.

Hessian Next on the list are hessian and scrim. These two much-used materials are both manufactured from jute in many qualities, weights, and widths. The most favoured width for upholstery work is 1·8m. (72in.). The heaviest quality hessian, called *tarpaulin*, is used on the best-class jobs as a covering over the springs, often termed *spring canvas*. Scrim is a more open type of hessian and the threads used in its manufacture are rounded in section, whereas the hessian threads are flat. Its major use is for covering the first stuffing of fibre or hair which is afterwards stitched into shape, hence the term 'scrim stuffing'.

Stuffings The principle stuffings used in traditional upholstery and moulded into shape by hand methods were fibre, hair, linsey wool—commonly termed black flock—kapok and feathers. Alva, a dried seaweed from the Baltic, was extensively used by the old-time upholsterer for the edges of the first stuffing. It was very easy to work when new, but became dusty and brittle with age. It was also affected by atmospheric

Fig. 1 Ball of twine and roll of webbing. Webbing is usually put up in 18yd. rolls.

13

conditions. Except when met with in an old repair job, it has quite faded away.

Horsehair is an excellent stuffing, although as in most things there are numerous qualities. The cheapest varieties consist of short hair with little resilience. Quite a lot in use at present is re-conditioned and contains a mixture of hoghair and hair other than that of the horse. Large quantities were imported from Russia and China, but lately most of it comes from America. It is washed and sterilized by various methods. After these processes it is twisted into rope, forming the curl which is retained throughout its life and supplying the resilience and springiness so essential. A large proportion is dyed black, whilst some is left its natural colour. These are called respectively black and grey hair, but the colour is not so important as the length and curl. The shorter the hair the less the curl, and therefore the less resilience and the greater the quantity required.

Occasionally dyed vegetable fibres are mixed with cheap-grade hair, making quite a useful mixture providing it is not sold as *all hair*. The term *all hair* should only be used where the stuffing contains nothing but the animal fibre.

Coming to the vegetable fibres one of the most popular is coco fibre, often called *ginger* fibre because of its colour. It is the lining of the coconut husk is prepared in several qualities. The best is a long fibre which has been curled similarly to hair, is usually free from dust, and is pleasant to work. The cheaper grades are not so long nor so clean, but make good stuffing for the cheaper class of work. The chief disadvantage of coco fibre is its tendency to break up and go to dust after years of use. It is also rather hard on the hands when being stitched into rolls.

Another much-used fibre is termed Algerian fibre. It is the split leaves of a dwarf Algerian palm known as *crin d'Afrique*. Some is dyed black and some left in its natural green colouring. Hence the term Black and Green fibre. The black seems to retain its curl better and it is softer and more resilient in use. The troublesome white mite has been found in the green fibre occasionally, so that most of it is treated by the importers to make it insect proof.

Flock, often called black wool, sometimes linsey wool, has always been extensively used in up-holstery. It is manufactured from rags and is the final stage of many a smart suit. The rags are washed and carded by machinery and rag flock must conform to the standards set up by the Rag Flocks Acts.

The felting process has been used with success on flock as on cotton, and felted flock or flock felt is much in demand, especially on spring-interior mattresses. It is easier to place a layer of felt in position than 'pick' loose stuffing evenly into place. As with most 'forms of stuffing there are various qualities, these being graded by the wool percentage of the rags used.

Stuffing pads Hair and fibre are all being woven onto hessian by a needle point process, thus making ready-made pads of stuffing. These pads can be obtained by the roll, or cut lengths, and have largely superseded the older method of building up a first stuffing of loose fillings, held in place by scrim or light hessian.

Rubberised hair is another layered product used on certain jobs. Linter's felt or *lintafelt* is also widely used in the place of wadding which it resembles. It consists of waste cotton linters felted together to form a thick type of wadding and put up in rolls of approx. 20 or so pounds, much used over hair and fibre and especially on spring interior mattresses.

In passing, mention might be made of kapok, a vegetable down from Java and the Dutch East Indies. Once much used for many types of cushions, also occasionally in mattresses. Very useful for life jackets and for seamen's bedding, because of its buoyancy and lightness. It was also used on the Antarctic and Arctic expeditions years ago because of its warmth and light weight. It may have been superseded by other materials now.

Feathers and down are graded in many qualities, the highest being real eiderdown. This is plucked from the breasts of the eider duck. As only a very small quantity can be obtained from each duck and it all has to be plucked by hand, it is very expensive.

Most of the down and feathers used by the trade are duck and common poultry feathers. The majority are imported from China and are washed and purified by the importers upon arrival.

Feather cushions When feather cushions are made up, the feathers must be contained in a feather-proof case. This is made from down-proof calico, and is a finely woven calico which has been waxed or treated to enable it to hold feathers and down.

Unbleached calico is sometimes used as a lining over the second stuffing before the final covering on good-class jobs, especially with hide work. In the past it was used much more frequently than at present, and it certainly helps a job to retain its shape. When the final stuffing is hair it is essential that a layer of wadding or linters felt is placed over the stuffing before covering. This is to prevent the hair working through the cover.

Wadding Wadding is made in two forms; sheet or pound wadding. The sheet variety is put up in bundles containing 12 yards and the other in pound packets, as its name implies. Some upholsterers prefer the pound wadding, others the sheet.

Tacks The ordinary blued, cut tack is the type most favoured. Various sizes are used for different materials, such as $\frac{5}{8}$in. improved for webbing, $\frac{3}{8}$in. and $\frac{1}{2}$in. improved for hessian, and $\frac{3}{8}$in. and $\frac{1}{2}$in. fine for various covers. The improved tack is cut larger than the fine and has a bigger head.

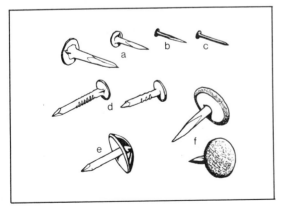

Fig. 2 Tacks, pins, nails and studs for upholstery. A Cut tacks in various sizes: B Cut gimp pin: C Wire gimp pin: D Clout nails: E Round head nail for finishing: F Fabric or leather-covered stud also used for finishing.

The majority of workshops carry a stock of the following sizes: $\frac{3}{8}$in. fine, $\frac{3}{8}$in. improved, $\frac{1}{2}$in. fine, $\frac{1}{2}$in. improved, and $\frac{5}{8}$in. improved; also $\frac{3}{8}$in. and $\frac{1}{2}$in. black cut gimp pins. One-inch steel clout nails or small wall nails are needed for patent springing.

Twines, etc. With the older methods of upholstery, twines and laid cord were essential sundries. A fairly thick twine is required for sewing the springs to the web, hence its name, springtwine. Another strong but finer twine is needed for various processes, such as stitching the rolls or edges, running through, etc. This is termed a stitching twine. Both spring and stitching twines are sold by the pound and generally put up in $\frac{1}{2}$lb. balls.

Laid cord is a much stouter twine or cord, and the yarns are *laid* together in such a manner as to prevent stretching. It is used to lace or lash the tops of the springs in position. Twines are made from Dutch, Flemish, Irish, and Russian flax and Italian and other hemp. Quality depends not only on the yarn but also on the method of manufacture. A cheap twine may weigh heavier and thus give less yardage to the ball.

Much modern upholstery is finished with piped seams. These are made by inserting a piece of piping cord, covered with the material being used, between the two portions of cover about to be stitched together. There are several varieties of piping cord on the market, one type being a cotton cord of various sizes put up in hanks or on reels. Another is made of compressed paper fibre and is much firmer than the cotton variety. Both have their special uses.

Silk, worsted, and cotton cords, gimps, and ruchings are still used for finishing soft cover work, but not so extensively as in the past. Leathercloth and hide jobs are generally finished with studs and bandings to match, or with antique-coppered, round-headed nails. These round-headed nails are also made in bright brass, antique brass, and chromium-plated finish.

Latex and chemical foam The arrival of Latex rubber foam, mainly as a cushion interior, started a new era in the trade. At first it was used for seat cushions, gradually edging out the spring interior cushion. Moulded cushions in a limited number of

Cutting squares and curves.

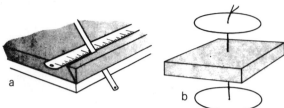

a

b

Use the edge of the bench and a steel straight edge as guides when cutting (a).
To cut circular or curved shapes cut two templates from hardboard and sandwich the foam with wire before cutting round the shapes (b).

Securing cushions.

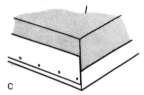

c

d

e

Straight edges (c) and curved edges (d and e) are made by glueing tape to foam cushions and then tacking in position. Hinges (f and g) can also be made from tape.

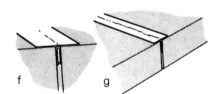

f

g

Domed shapes.

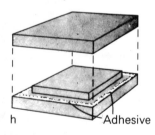

h

Adhesive

Curved seats.

Adhesive

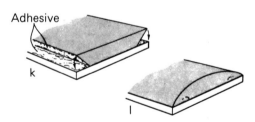

k

l

Padded backs.

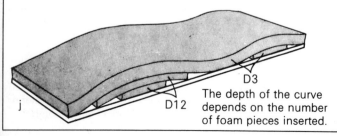

j

D3

D12

The depth of the curve depends on the number of foam pieces inserted.

Rounded edges.

Adhesive

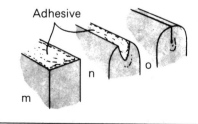

m

n

o

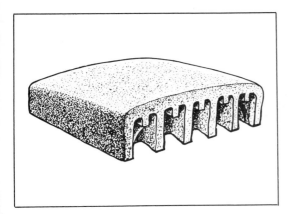

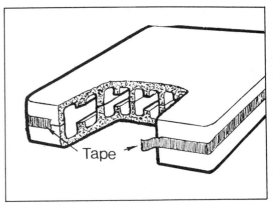

Fig. 3 Section through moulded latex cushioning. Although initial cost may be greater than other materials, the time saved in their uses saves much expense.

Fig. 4 Latex foam cushion. This is usually made by joining two moulded shapes together with solution and taping the seams.

sizes came first, then hand-built cushions, squabs and many different shapes and sizes were made up. As the industry grew the number of ready-moulded sizes and shapes increased. Sheets of solid foam, cavity foam and pinhole foam in many sizes and qualities became available. Also adhesives for making secure joints were produced. Foam latex rubber has never been a cheap production as compared with fibre, flock and even horsehair, but less labour is required to form the finished upholstered article. Its resilience is first rate and durability very good, providing it is covered and protected from strong light. A moulded latex cushion is shown in section in Fig. 3. See also Fig. 4. During the past few years chemical experiment and progress has resulted in the production of synthetic foams. These are less costly than the latex foam but also less resilient and slower to regain their shape.

There are many grades, densities and firmness. Also they are more resistant to light and damage by chemical action. Since the early days the improvements in performance has been so great that its use as a filling has created quite a revolution, especially at the cheaper end of the trade.

It is produced in many densities and hardness in sheet or block form from 6·25mm. ($\frac{1}{4}$in.) thickness upwards. 3in., $3\frac{1}{2}$in., 4in., and 6in. thick blocks are cut to shape for cushions, squabs, boat cushions,

bar seats, etc. Moulded shapes for cushions, stool tops, pillows, and many other items are, or can be, made. The making of special moulds can be expensive unless many shapes are needed. Arms and backs do not require such heavy density foam as seats. In fact, there has been a tendency to use very light density cushions on the backs of many productions.

Reconstituted foam is a further development. Off-cuts from the blocks, sheets and other wastage is shredded into small pieces and mixed with new liquid foam and recured. This forms a firmer foam which has many uses.

A further development which has made big inroads into the older methods and much used with both the foams is rubber webbing. Several makes and qualities are available and the types with a fabric core similar to motor tyre construction are the most durable. The combination of either latex or polyether foam with rubber webbing can be used to give quite a streamlined effect to many designs. Methods of fixing rubber webbing vary according to the job in hand. On a production where the fixing is not seen they can be stapled, tacked or fixed with small clout nails.

Another method much used on fireside chairs is for the rails to be grooved, the webbing cut to size and fitted with metal ends. The ends are pushed

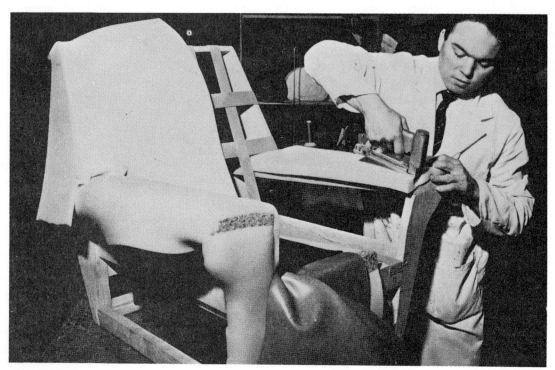

Above: Stapling foam to the frame of a chair. *Dunlop.*

Below: Fabricating seats from a combination of latex foam and polyether foams. *Dunlop.*

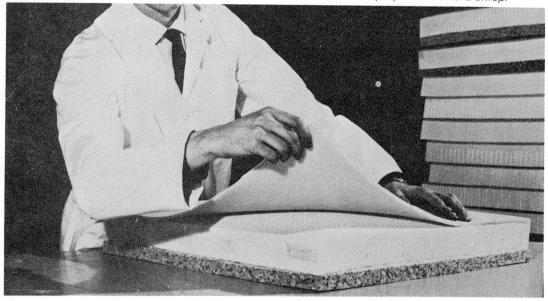

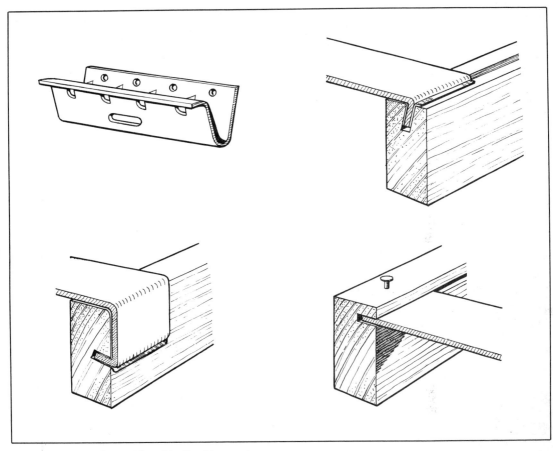

Fig. 5 Methods of attaching *Pirelli* rubber webs.

into the grooves and are held there by the angle or a small nail is driven through a hole in the metal. See Fig. 5.

Whatever method is used for fixing approx. a 10% stretch is needed on seats. On small seats the webbing is rarely checked, just five or six pieces of web fixed one way across the seat space. This is all right for an average weight, but where any heavy weight is likely to use a chair or settee, two or three cross webs checked under and over make a better job.

Chapter four

Springs and Springing

The traditional method of obtaining comfortable seating was to use various sizes and gauges of coil springs sewn with twine on to a webbing base. The tops of the springs were laced together with strong laid cord from back to front and side to side, so keeping the springs in their correct position. The end product produced by a good tradesman, fitted the body in all positions and gave lasting comfort, but it took skill and time to achieve.

Many prefabricated units for seats and backs have been produced, usually grouped together and loosely termed *patent springing* by the trade. Single-spring units consisting of a number of springs riveted to a base of steel laths formed the simplest type as in Fig. 1. The number of both

Fig. 1 Single sprung chair seat (Siddall and Hilton Ltd.)

Fig. 2 Tension sprung base chair seat (Siddall and Hilton Ltd.)

Fig. 3 Reverse side of tension sprung base chair seat (Siddall and Hilton Ltd.)

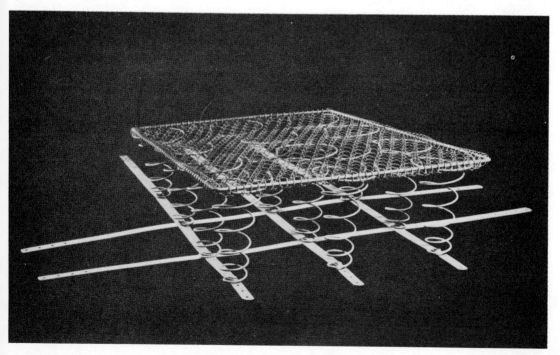

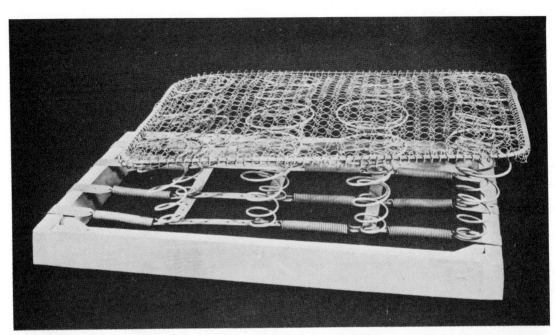

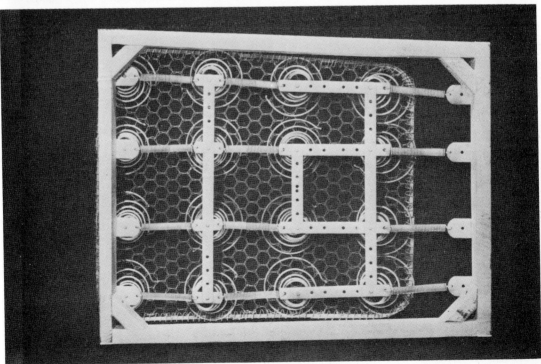

springs and laths varied according to the size and quality of the unit.

A better quality has three laths each way and nine springs, one riveted at each crossing point. The top coils of the springs are woven into a lace wire mesh which holds them in position, thereby doing the same work as the laid cord in a hand-sprung job. This wire mesh covering also forms a good base for the stuffing to rest upon.

Double-Spring Unit One type of patent spring-ing which has proved very successful and popular consists of short laths linked together with tension springs. These short strips are joined widthways by laths running the full width of the unit. Coil springs about 5in. in height are fixed where the laths cross by riveting. Their tops are held in position by a wire mesh on a wire frame, or a flat steel tape frame which in turn is held in position with fine coiled spring wire. The front springs are

stapled to the front rail of the frame and the back lath pieces nailed to the back rail. The short tension springs give a comfortable seating position.

Double-Sprung unit A popular form of double-sprung unit also has the steel laths for a base, with the bottom layer of springs riveted to the laths. A wire mesh holds the top coils of these springs in place, also taking the bottom coils of the top layer. The top coils of this layer are kept in position by a second piece of wire mesh. Most of the meshes are woven on a wire frame so that a firm edge is formed all round the unit. Slight variations of this type are often met with.

Coil springs Before leaving this subject mention must be made of the ordinary common or garden variety of upholstery spring, which has stood the test of many years of service. It is a double cone, vertical coil spring obtainable in many sizes and gauges. The sizes most used and generally stocked are: 4in. by 13 gauge; 5in. by 10 gauge and 12 gauge; 6in. by 10 gauge and 12 gauge; 7in. by 9 gauge; 8in. by 9 gauge; 9in. by 8 gauge or 9 gauge; 10in. by 8 gauge.

Fig. 4 *Serpentine* base chair seat, this is very new and the last word in comfort (Siddall and Hilton Ltd.)

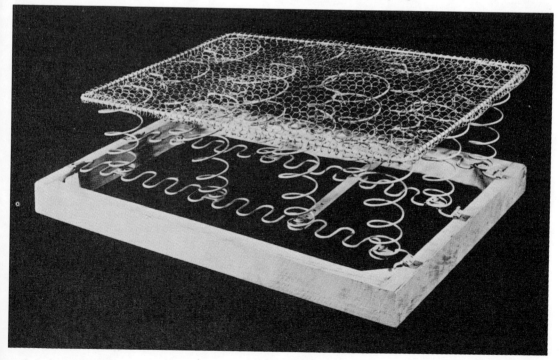

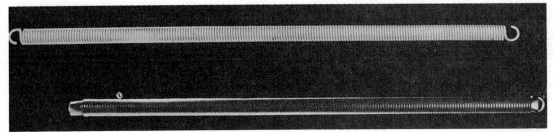

Fig. 6 Tension springs for fireside chair.

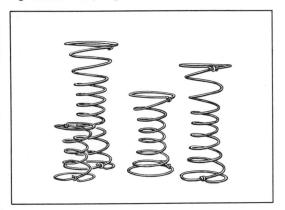

Fig. 5 Examples of ordinary coil springs.
These are the types used in hand-sprung work.

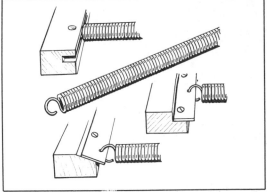

Fig. 7 Tension or cable springs and their attachments.
The method of attachment must be ascertained before frame is made as groove rebate or chamfers may be required.

The smaller sizes and lighter gauges are used on backs and arms and the others for seats. The smaller the gauge number the stouter the wire. Fig. 5 shows some coil springs.

When deciding what size and gauge of spring to use much depends upon the quality of stuffing and the class of job. The majority of springs and spring units are made from copper-covered steel wire, but many are also made from black japanned and galvanized steel wire. Springs singly or as made-up units probably form the most important single item making for comfort and durability of any upholstered article. Once again quality counts.

Tension springs Tension or cable springs used in conjunction with cushions on seats have been a useful addition to seat springing. As the name implies, the spring wire is tightly wound in the form of a cable, $\frac{1}{2}$in. or $\frac{3}{8}$in. diameter as in Fig. 6. Tension springs are fixed to the side of a chair frame by engaging a link or hook at each end over a nail, screw, or screw eye. Some manufacturers use a metal plate which is drilled at approx. 2 in. intervals to take a required number of springs and can be screwed to the frame. Seat springs of $\frac{1}{2}$in. diameter usually require a tension of 1 inch to the foot when fixing. Back springs of $\frac{3}{8}$in. diameter are much lighter and require rather more tension. Where the actual fixing is not seen it can be done with clout nails, small wall nails, or staples, etc. Fig. 7 shows several alternative methods of fixing. Grooves, rebates or chamfers will have to be made on the rails before the frame is assembled.

When a loose cushion is required a platform over the springs is made from a lining or other suitable material to tone with the covering material. One

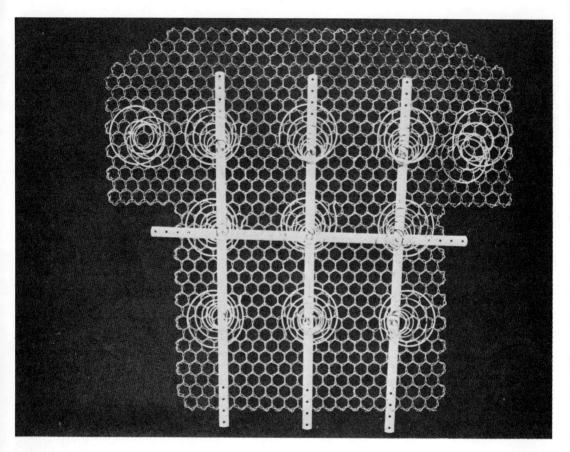

Fig. 8 Mesh covered back spring unit (Siddall and Hilton Ltd.).

method is to enclose each spring in a pocket sewn on the lining. Another way is to make two pockets only, one at the front and one at the back of the platform lining. To do this insert the rear spring into its pocket and fix it in position. Bring the platform over the other springs already fixed, and insert the front but one spring into the front pocket. To cover the front spring and front rail, tack one edge of the cover to the top of the front rail. Pass the other end under and then over the first spring. Before returning it to the front rail, lay a piece of wadding or linter's felt along the space between the spring and the front edge of the rail. Bring the cover over the whole and tack it to the underside of the front rail. These are the methods frequently used on fireside easy chairs.

Feather cushion Feather cushions were extensively used before the advent of spring interiors. Properly filled with good-quality feathers they give years of comfortable service. An inside case of down-proof calico is required for feather or down cushions. The down-proof case would be cut about 25mm. (1in.) larger all round than the outer case. It should be divided into compartments, thus helping to keep the feathers where they are most required. For example, a cushion 500mm. (20in.) wide by 600mm. (24in.) deep would have three compartments, the front and middle ones being well filled but the back one not quite so full.

Be generous when cutting the divisions, which can be of either down-proof or ordinary calico. Allow about 50mm. (2in.) more in depth than the outside border, as there is a tendency to drag down which will show too distinctly on the outer case.

Fig. 9 Combination of tension springs for seat.
Serpentine springs for back (Siddall and
Hilton Ltd.)

A further addition to the various types of springing is the *No-sag*; *Zig-zag* and similar brands of springs built up on the circular arc principle. The wire is made in a serpentine strip then formed and tempered in a perfect circle. After being cut to the required size the spring is stretched and anchored between two points. This makes the permanent arc which gives it resiliency and strength. The springs are equally spaced on seats or backs and connected to each other with wire links. The two outside springs are connected to the side rails with $\frac{1}{2}$in. diameter helical springs. Seats require heavier gauge wire than backs. An average back spring would be about 12 gauge, likewise a seat about $8\frac{1}{2}$ to 9 gauge. Fig. 9 shows the use of serpentine springs for a chair back.

It is difficult to place rubber webbing as it is not a spring but a resilient webbing made up in various combinations of rubber and fabric. In its better qualities it is a strong and durable product, extremely useful for many seating problems and backs. It is made in various widths from 12·5mm. ($\frac{1}{2}$in.) to 62·5 ($2\frac{1}{2}$in.) and usually a 10% tension is required when fixing. There are many ways of fixing according to whether it is seen or unseen. It can be tacked directly on to a wooden frame with tacks or small clout nails.

The length required can be cut to the required size and the ends fitted with metal clips which are inserted into grooves cut in the frame rails. One advantage it has over tension springs when used on the inexpensive types of fireside easies, is that it does not mark the undersides of cushions. Of course a lining cover stitched up with a half inch thickness of foam inserted will obviate, this, but when price is the main concern this lining is omitted. A feature common to all the horizontal springs and webbing suspended between two points is that they help the designer to use more shallow surfaces. This also makes for lightness which again pleases.

Below: Three-seater sofa. Fully sprung upholstery with deep-buttoned back and pure latex rubber seat cushioning. *G-Plan*.

Chapter five

Frames

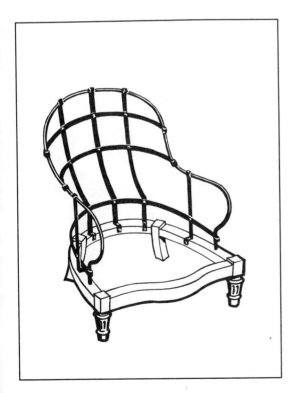

Upholstered chairs and settees are built up on *frames*. This is the term used to describe the skeleton of wood or metal which is the foundation for the upholstery. Until the post-war shortage of timber brought about the development of metal frames practically all stuff-over upholstery frames were constructed of hardwood.

The use of metal in frames is not new. An early predecessor of the metal frame was the *iron-back* easy chair, one of the most comfortable types of upholstered easy chairs ever made, see Fig. 1. The base, or seat frame, and legs were of hardwood, and an iron rod bent in a continuous sweep formed the outline of the back and arms. This rod was held in place and supported by metal laths about an inch in width, these being bent over the rod and riveted at their crossing points, then screwed or nailed to the wood seat rails. This method of construction gave a springiness to the back which combined with a 'fit your back' curve made for a high degree of comfort.

Wood frames To return to the majority of frames of timber construction, good, sound Quebec birch is the ideal. Beech, oak, chestnut, ash, maple, and off-cuts of many other hardwoods are sometimes used. Modern practice is to use dowels for most joints in frame making, though an antique or early Victorian frame may have had mortise-and-tenon joints. Properly glued and correctly fitting dowels combined with carefully cut joints will make a good, sound frame. The main seat rails on large easies, settees, and other big jobs require four dowels to each joint. On smaller chairs, etc., three are sufficient. Two dowels on the arm and back joints are general, but each joint must be judged on its merits: whether the rails are wide or narrow, and taking into account the stresses they may have to bear. Tacking rails are frequently fixed with a single dowel at one end and housed into an upright at the other end, then screwed or nailed.

Fig. 1 The old iron back, now obsolete but much sought after by Victoriana collectors. A successful Victorian effort in comfort. This is a relic of the days when an upholsterer needed more than a mouthful of tacks and a hammer or a stapling gun.

Fig. 2 Tub easy chair.
This is generally 625mm. (2ft. 1in.) by 625mm.
(2ft. 1in.) and upwards in size.

A frame should, to a large extent, conform to the general outline of the finished upholstery. One frame may, however, form the basis of several designs by the addition of extension pieces and so on. When constructing a frame several points must be considered: height of seat from the floor; height of arms; whether springs will be used on the arms, whether a spring edge to the seat is required; are double-sprung units going to be used?

Sizes The height of the seat from the ground should be in proportion to the length of the seat from front to back. Thus a large easy, intend for lounging and having a long seat, needs to be low, about 325–350mm. (13–14in.) from the ground to the top of the front edge. A chair intended for upright sitting and having a short seat from front to back would be between 375mm. and 425mm. (15 and 17in.) in height at the front. The arms and backs are likewise proportioned to the seat. If sprung arms are required the top arm rail must be set lower to allow for the height of the springs.

On a deep-sprung, webbed base, spring-edge job, double front rails and double tacking rails all round

Fig. 3 Victorian-type easy frame.

Fig. 4 Plain reproduction frame.

28

Fig. 5 Reproduction wing easy frame.

Fig. 6 Wing easy frame.

are preferable. A frame intended for a double-spring unit does not need the double tacking rails and according to the unit construction may not require two front rails. The bottom seat rails of a frame on which it is intended to fix a spring unit on a lath base can have 1⅛in. by 3in. instead of 1¾in. by 2in. rails. There is not the same stress on these rails as when web is used. Corner blocks or braces are advisable on all frames.

Settee frames require a stout main front rail, especially the larger sizes. A centre stretcher rail is necessary on all the smaller settees and sometimes two are required on the larger types. Special springing systems may require additional rails, but the general construction is the same. Drop ends to the settee frames were popular up to the change in style from the scroll arm to the square-arm design. Since then they have almost faded out. Properly constructed they were very useful, although often a source of annoyance to the upholsterer, being awkward to get at and to finish cleanly.

At one time there were numerous metal actions available, many of them patented or registered ideas. In spite of this, variations of the wooden ratchet principle were much favoured, possibly because of cheapness and ease of manufacture through having the timber on the spot. Some of the metal actions were quite good and serviceable. One of the simplest was worked on the principle of a round rod passing through a hole at an angle. A metal plate with a hole slightly larger than the rod was screwed to a movable wooden rail. As the rail was moved by a lever worked by the hand or foot (the lever projected through the outside cover) the rod passed through the hole in an upright position. When the lever was released a spring brought the rail over so that the edges of the hole gripped the rod at an angle, thus holding it rigid.

As the design of upholstered furniture changes so must the frame upon which it is built. Wood is still the basis of much upholstery but moulded shapes of various materials are challenging its position. One of these is fibreglass reinforced polyurethane foam, moulded shapes. Chairs developed by rotational moulding of polythene foam and many types of shells in polyurethane foam have come to the fore. Many of them are fixed to a wood or metal pedestal base, and revolve or rock (or do

Fig. 8 Winged settee frame.

Fig. 7 Contemporary frame.

Fig. 9 Chesterfield settee frame.

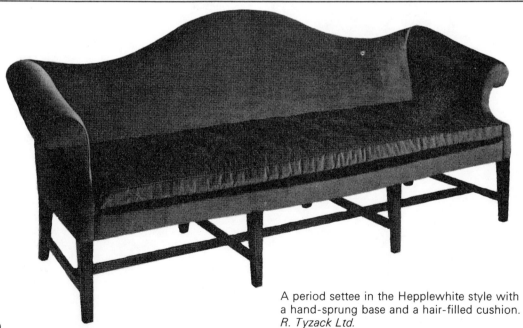

A period settee in the Hepplewhite style with a hand-sprung base and a hair-filled cushion. *R. Tyzack Ltd.*

both) at a gentle touch. Most of these moulded shapes are well-curved and the covers used are of the stretch, knitted nylon fabrics which cling to the curves without too much fixing. The curves are moulded to take the shape of the body so the foam used is not very thick in depth, and, although cushions are needed in many designs, the final product is much lighter than the more traditional frames. The fixing of the foam and covers on these jobs brings into use rubber adhesives, stapling, zippers, and *Velcro* fastening.

The bespoke trade and the reproduction work will probably require wood frames of sound construction for many years. Also the homeworker will surely get pleasure from making up his own designs in natural timber. At the cheaper end of the trade where the job is fully mass-produced, many of the frames are made up in sections. Two separate arms, seat and back. These are upholstered separately, then assembled and bolted or screwed together before finishing the outsides and fitting the bottom and castors. Thus the upholsterer must use his skill to build up comfort and an attractive appearance upon many different types of bases.

All the photographs of chair frames in this chapter were kindly lent by H. Vaughan Ltd.

Chapter six

General Principles and Useful Hints

Generally speaking, large upholstery jobs involve the same principles as small ones, and we give here some of the chief points to be noted when carrying out the various operations.

Webbing Webbing forms the basis of most hand-sprung work. It must be tightly stretched across the space it covers. The strands are interchecked, thus supporting and being supported by each other and so ensuring maximum strength. In most cases webbing should be tacked on with five tacks spaced as shown in the various illustrations in this book, three and two. These tacks are driven through the doubled-over web at the starting end. At the finishing end four tacks slightly staggered are used. These are driven through the single thickness of web and the web is trimmed off about 25mm. (1in.) beyond them. This inch of spare web is turned back over the tacks and fastened down with two tacks.

Tacking methods The tacking off or tacking down of various materials constitutes a large part of upholstery work. Web, hessian, and all materials that are likely to take a strain should be doubled

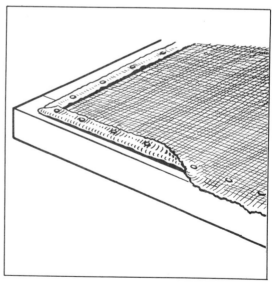

Fig. 1 How to tack off hessian.
Note how the edge is doubled over.

Left: A comfortable and successful wing easy in the modern style. *G-Plan.*

over when tacking off. In this way the top layer of material acts as a buffer between the tack head and the second or main piece of fabric, see Fig. 1.

Where neatness alone is the objective the edges are doubled under as they do not take a heavy strain. Examples are the cover on various parts of the job, hessian or calico bottoms, and the scrim covering of the first stuffing. Hide and other real leathers are left raw-edged in many instances, as when finished close up to show-wood or when the edge is covered with a banding. Leathercloth can often be treated in the same manner, but not if the cotton backing is likely to show.

When tacking on outside arms, backs, etc. it is usual to avoid showing the heads of the tacks or staples.

The method employed is termed *back tacking*. To do this place the piece of cover in position fixing it with two or three temporary tacks driven through from the back of the cover. Drive these home when correctly placed.

Take a strip of cardboard or buckram 12·5mm. (½in.) wide and tack it along the edge of the cover in position. When completed the cover can be turned down, fixed temporarily along the sides, and tacked off at the bottom. This leaves the tacks unseen at the top whilst the sides can be slip stitched, gimp pinned or stapled.

Twine work Sewing with various thicknesses of twine used in several types of needles enters into many operations in upholstery. Thus knots and ties play an important part in the build-up of upholstery. Most sewing operations are started with a slip-knot. One of the most useful forms of this knot is shown in Fig. 3. When sewing springs to the webbing start with a slip-knot, followed by the simple half-hitch, shown in Figs. 4 and 5. The process is completed at the last point with a double hitch, and the twine is knotted before cutting off the surplus.

The same method is used when sewing the top coils of the springs to the spring hessian or canvas, as it is sometimes termed. Lacing or the lashing together of the top coils of the springs is done with a laid cord, a form of heavy twine specially made, or laid, to prevent stretching. Two methods of making the tie around the coil of the spring are in general use. One is a hitch, as shown in Fig. 6A.

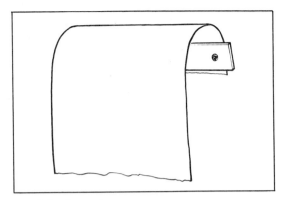

Fig. 2 Back-tacking.

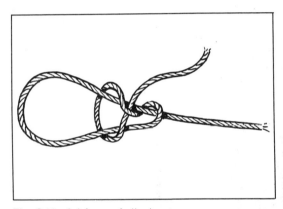

Fig. 3 Useful form of slip-knot.

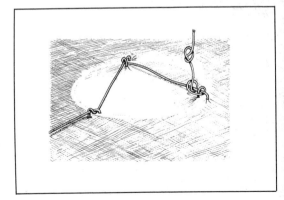

Fig. 4 Sewing top of spring to the hessian. Half-hitches are generally used and a double hitch when finishing.

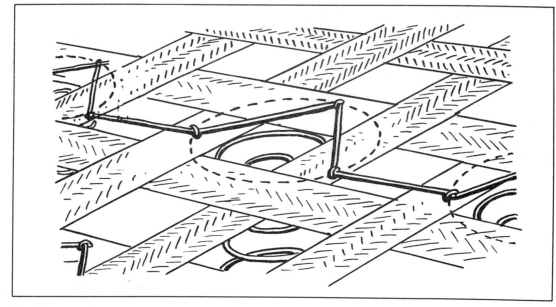

Fig. 5 Underside of webbed seat showing method of sewing springs to webbing.

By using this tie it is fairly simple to adjust the position of the spring if desired. The alternative method is a single knot, B. This is difficult to alter, but it is more secure.

Stitching the roll or edge is another operation started with a slip-knot. It is continued with a series of twists made round the needle. These pull into a tie as the needle is withdrawn, see Fig. 7. A single twist is sufficient when making the sink, or blind stitch and for any intermediate stitching. The top or final stitch should always be pulled very tight and by making a double twist will remain taut as the stitching is continued. At the end of a row of stitching the final stitch is completed by knotting the twine before cutting it off.

Cutting materials The usual method of keeping a straight line when cutting hessian or scrim is by withdrawing a thread. This leaves a wide space between the two adjoining threads which gives an easy mark to follow.

Calico and most cotton materials tear easily both ways, warp and weft. P.V.C. fabrics can be marked with a pencil and cut with the scissors.

This is probably the safest way. Patterned materials can usually be cut by following the pattern through. In all difficult cases use a straight-edge and a piece of tailor's chalk.

Filling materials Fibre or hair is the usual first or scrim stuffing; fibre generally because it is much cheaper than hair. These are used because they are easily stitched into shape to form a roll or edge that is both even and firm. Black flock or wool and hair are the top stuffings; wool because it is cheaper in price and does the job reasonably well; hair because it is resilient and retains the spring much longer than other natural stuffings. A layer of wadding or linters' felt is required over hair before the final cover, otherwise the hair will work through the covering.

Fixing tacks Temporarily fixing covers, hessian etc., in place with partly driven tacks is common custom. It enables the material to be gradually worked into position. Some operations in covering may need several fixings before they are finally tacked off, hence the need for only partly driven tacks. They can be easily lifted as the work proceeds.

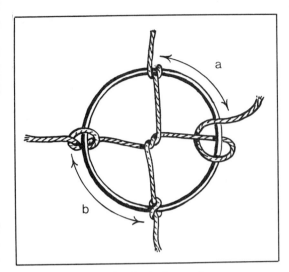

Fig. 6 Alternative ties for lacing springs.
A is the easier to regulate: B the more secure.

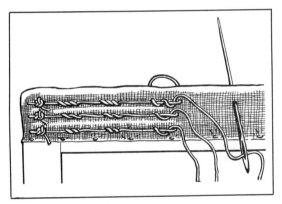

Fig. 7 Stitching a roll or edge.

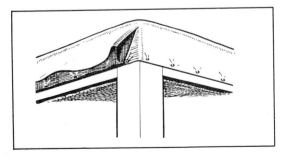

Fig. 8 Single pleat for square corner.

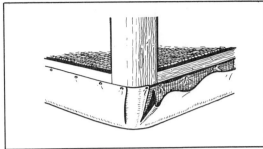

Fig. 9 Rounded corner with double pleat.

Fig. 10 Cutting cover around show-wood surface.

Treatment of corners Sometimes it is difficult to know the correct treatment for a corner. As a general rule a rounded corner needs a double pleat, Fig. 9, whilst a sharp or square corner requires a single pleat, Fig. 8. The main object with all corners is to keep the top part of the pleat or pleats below the top surface. Otherwise it gives an ugly finish, wears badly, and is poor workmanship.

Fitting the cover round show-wood arms, uprights, etc. There are often occasions when a cover must be cut to fit neatly to some polished wood. Turn the cover back away from the polished surface so the fold of the cover just touches the wood. Mark with chalk or pencil a line from the outer edge of the cover to the point where the fold touches the wood and cut along this line. Sometimes a double cut will be needed as on a fireside chair where the polished arms adjoin an upholstered back. Practice is needed with most jobs, but these few tips should assist in keeping to the right lines.

Chapter seven

Planning and Cutting Covers

The planning and cutting of the material for covering a chair or settee need care and forethought if they are to be done in an efficient and economical manner. The covering is usually the most expensive single item used in an upholstered article. Therefore the saving of a quarter or half yard of material is well worth while. Soft covers, such as moquette, tapestries, linens, damasks, etc., can often be joined in inconspicuous places and material saved. With P.V.C. coated fabrics, joins must be avoided. The cutting of hides and morocco skins will be dealt with later.

Patterned material Before bringing the scissors into action carefully consider the pattern (if any) of the material. If it is a large, centred design, such as a medallion, or a bunch or vase of flowers, it is necessary to centre the most prominent features of the pattern on the seats and inside backs. Stripes also call for special treatment; they must be either centred or balanced on the seat and back, and paired on the arms. If possible this should be carried out on the outside arms and outside backs as well. Sometimes this would mean too extravagant a use of covering material, but aim to work them as symmetrically as possible. In fact, whatever the design of the cover, whether large, small, striped, or all-over pattern, always strive for regularity of design, thus giving a pleasing finish to the work.

Joining The object of a good cutter, then, is to lay out his material with as few joins and as little waste as possible. The joins should be matched unless they are going to be placed in a very inconspicuous position. Some materials present greater difficulties in sewing than others. A tapestry or damask will often join up with the seam hardly noticeable if the pattern is carefully matched, whereas a plain velvet or moquette rarely looks really well when joined.

Moquettes, velvets, and pile fabrics in general shade according to the direction of the pile. You can liken this to a cat's fur. If you brush it the wrong way it shows a different shade. This must always be remembered with these materials, and it is advisable to make certain of the direction of the pile before any cuts are made. A good plan is to mark the back of the whole roll or piece that is being used with a series of T's or arrows on each side of the centre line, i.e. on each half width.

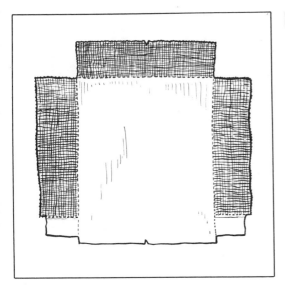

Fig. 1 Seat cover flyed to economize material. The fly is of less expensive but strong material and is used in concealed places.

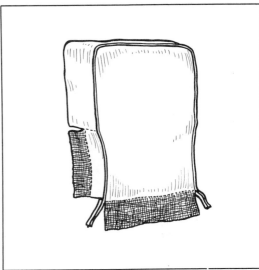

Fig. 2 Back cover cut to fit around arms. Note the flys.

Flys The term flys or flying up is used for the odd pieces of lining, casement cloth, hessian, or any odd cuttings which are sewn to the cover to save material where it is not seen, Fig. 1. Thus the seat would be flyed on the three sides where it disappears under the arms and the back, likewise the inside arms and the inside back.

At the point where the arms merge into the back, the inside back cover is cut to fit over the arms and a collar or gusset-piece inserted and sewn as in Fig. 2. This is often omitted on cheaper jobs, but makes a snug, neat finish. With hide and P.V.C. fabrics the gusset is essential in order to obtain a clean finish, and requires accurate cutting. A piece of piping is inserted in most of these hard cover jobs, and, although this is not so frequently used on soft cover jobs, it is an improvement well worth the trouble. Fig. 3 shows how the piping is made.

The terms used for the various pieces of cover are: seat, inside back, outside back, inside arm, outside arm, and front facings, the latter being the pieces of cover on the front of scroll or similar shaped arms. Back facings are similar pieces on the sides of the back. The front border is the front

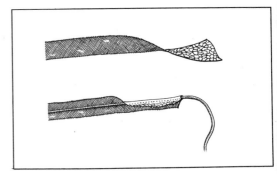

Fig. 3 How piping is made with inserted cord. The piping strips should be cut on the bias or cross whenever possible.

portion finishing the seat. Back borders are the finish to a square or shaped back, usually continuing from one arm to the other.

Planning and cutting covers In the past furnishing cords and gimps were used to cover the finishing points of facings and borders on soft covers. These methods take time and skill to use

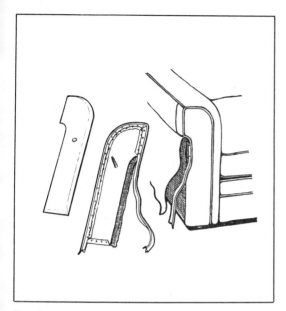

Fig. 4 How a wood facing is covered and fitted. Note the bolt which passes through the front arm.

Remove the facing from the frame and insert the bolt in the facing if it is likely to be difficult to get at after covering. Cover the facing with a piece of the material, leaving the outside edge untacked. Tack a piece of piping all round, but leave it hanging loose on the outside edge. Replace the facing on the job and bolt down tightly. Next, tack the edge which has been left loose, also the piping, finishing off the outside arm or back up to the piping.

Another method, often used is to cut the required shape in thin ply or hardboard, and use staples or $\frac{1}{4}$in. tacks to fix the cover all round. Tack off the outside arm or back on the front of the frame and place the covered facing over it. Hold it in place and using the point of the regulator spread the weave of the cover. Drive home an inch panel pin through the opening of the cover. Use several panel pins to make sure of a good fixing and push the weave back in place. This method should only be used on soft or other suitable covers which will not show the insertion.

successfully and do not fit in very well with present day practice and covering materials. Piping of facings and borders has been very popular and makes a good finish. Ruching is another method and is highly decorative.

It is best to avoid the use of either of the above finishes on the front of arms and other places where they come in for a lot of conscious or subconscious rubbing. Plain seams have become regular practice on many jobs partly because of this, and also because the thickness of piped seams under the cover when used over foam does not bed into the foam to the same extent as they would into the older loose fillings.

Wood facings A neat finish to P.V.C. fabrics and hide work is obtained by wood facings covered with the material being used, as shown in Fig. 4. Make templates of stiff paper or cardboard and cut the required shapes from ply or other available wood. These facings are usually fixed into place with one or two bolts. Fix them temporarily with a nail or two, then bore through the facings and the frame. Countersink the hole to take the head of the bolt.

Cutting Now for the actual cutting of the material. In most small workshops where nearly every job is different from the last the upholsterer usually cuts his own covers. The measurements are taken with a tape measure when the chair has reached the first, or scrim, stuffing stage, or the calico stage if this is being used over the top stuffing. Fig. 5 shows where the measurements are taken. Tuck the end of the tape between the seat and back just out of sight, and draw the remainder over the seat to the front edge of the point where the piping should finish. Allow 20–25mm. ($\frac{3}{4}$–1in.) on this measurement for sewing.

On all materials that are closely woven and unlikely to unravel, 9·4mm. ($\frac{3}{8}$in.) is sufficient for joins and seams. Loosely woven and thick pile fabrics require a full 12·5mm. ($\frac{1}{2}$in.), occasionally more. Next measure over the inside back from the bottom to the top, allowing about 25mm. (1in.) for sewing and tacking off. Add a further 25–36mm. (1–1$\frac{1}{2}$in.) to both these measurements for the top stuffing if measuring over the scrim.

The method of dealing with the width measurements is somewhat different. In the majority of types of chairs a half width of 50in. material will be sufficient for the seats. This also applies to quite a number of designs for inside backs. A full width is needed on all two-seater settees inside and outside backs and often more, involving two joins. In some cases a width alone of material will suffice for the settee seat. Three-seater settees will need at least a width and a half on the backs and often more. Sometimes when using plain fabrics it may be advisable to change the method of cutting from across the width to along the width. Plan your cuts first and check for shading on all fabrics. Always use velvet with the pile brushing downwards. Joins should be equally spaced at each end whether a plain or patterned material is used.

The only exception to this rule is when using a small all-over patterned or plain material on a fluted or buttoned surface where the join can be hidden. It is best wherever possible to keep to the rule of joining at each end, thus equalizing the strain on the join as well as obtaining a balanced finish.

Arm measurements The inside arms are also measured from the meeting-place of arms and seat. There are many shapes and types of arms and each must be treated according to type. A scroll arm is measured over to the underside of the top arm rail for the inside arm, and from there to the underside of the seat rail for the outside arm.

The width measurements also call for discretion as to whether half or whole widths should be used. With scroll arms whole widths can often be planned to cover the inside arms, using the pieces left over for the joins on the front and outside backs of the settee, outside arms, facings, etc. For the outside arms the use of half widths with a join placed at the rear end of the arm is usually the most economical treatment for this type.

With the modern variety, however, the reverse often gives the best finish, that is, a half width with a join on the inside arm and a whole width on the outside. The outside back of an easy chair requires a half width, and the settee outside back a whole width with small joins. Most of the foregoing remarks apply to 50in. or 'double width' material. Single width material or 31in., of course, involves more joins on the larger surfaces. Settee seats will require two and sometimes three widths, likewise the inside and outside backs. The same rule applies; make these joins away from the centre line. For instance, take a settee seat requiring two widths of 31in. material. Split one width down the centre and

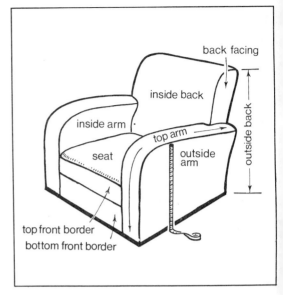

Fig. 5 Method of measuring for the cover. This shows the various sections and shows where the sizes are measured.

join at the selvedges on each side of the remaining full width, carefully matching the pattern.

Cushions The boxed border, feather-filled, foam-filled, or latex foam cushion is much used in present-day upholstery. Cutting the cover for these is not difficult. Make a template or pattern of stiff paper or cardboard if there are many curves to consider, and cut to that, allowing 9·4—12·5mm. ($\frac{3}{8}$—$\frac{1}{2}$in.) all round for turnings. If a fairly square or oblong cushion is required measure the space in the ordinary manner and add the sewing allowances.

The borders for a feather cushion can be cut about 106·25mm. (4$\frac{1}{4}$in.) in depth, thus finishing approximately 87·5mm. (3$\frac{1}{2}$in.) in depth. This makes a pleasing finish, neither too skimpy nor too fat for the average suite. With a foam-filled cushion the depth must be regulated according to the thickness of the foam.

When making a cushion-seated settee or easy chair it is customary to use a lining or cheaper material on the platform seat. This is the portion of the seat 100, 125, 150mm. (4, 5 or 6in.) from the front edge that is entirely covered by the cushions. On soft-covered jobs this saves about 1·2m. (4ft.) of 50in. material on the suite. On hide and leather-cloth jobs it is not only economical but necessary, since the cushions would otherwise slide about.

When making piping the material should be cut on the bias or on the cross, as it is more often termed — i.e. diagonally across the cover. This allows it to 'give' or stretch when made up, thus setting better on the job.

Allowances must be made for the amount of full-ness required when cutting for a buttoned or fluted job. It is better to err on the generous side in these cases, as nothing looks worse than a strained finish with this class of work. The old proverb, look before you leap, can be translated into, think before you cut, and is sound advice.

In the past there has been a wide range of fabrics available for upholstery in numerous qualities from hand-made silk velvet to cotton and the cheaper man-made fibres.

During the last few years, great progress has been made in the manufacture of man-made fibres and some very nice materials have emerged. *Antron, Crilon, Elvan, Dralon,* Nylons and Rayons have all contributed to a much wider range of covering materials.

Below: This three piece suite is sculptured in African teak and has reversible seat and back cushions. *McGregor of Scotland.*

Chapter eight

Hides and Moroccos

Hide or, as the layman usually calls it, 'real leather' upholstery has been popular for many years. Hide is the shortened term used to classify cowhides. These are large skins covering an area of 45–55 or even more square feet. Moroccos are the smaller skins of goats. Roans are sheep-skins roughly the same size as the moroccos.

Amongst the old-timers in the peace and plenty era of the early part of this century morocco-covered upholstery was regarded as the highest grade of work. Today moroccos are rarely used, but when they are they still require the highest degree of skill from the upholsterer.

Morocco skins are specially selected goats' skins, the best coming from the mountainous districts of Middle Europe, cheaper grades being from Persia, India, and other warmer countries. The goats live a very hardy life and have little fat or grease in their skins, hence their splendid wearing qualities. Thirty and even forty years in constant use is not uncommon.

A fine reproduction easy chair buttoned in hide.
R. Tysack Ltd.

Moroccos often remain serviceable and retain much of their natural beauty for that period. Roans were used in conjunction with moroccos, the goat-skins being used on the fronts of the work in hand and the sheep-skins on the outsides. Roans have nothing like the durability of moroccos. Their place is generally taken by a piece of P.V.C. fabric in present-day practice. Cowhides gained in popularity soon after the 1914–18 war. The skins are cheaper per square foot than moroccos; also, being larger, they have a greater cutting area, thus giving less waste. They are durable, although not quite so long-lived in use as a morocco skin. Modern dyes and finishing methods have produced some fine, soft, and beautiful hides.

There are several grades and qualities, the two classes most used by the trade being termed full-grain hides and buffed hides. Buffed hides are those which have some defects and have been buffed over with carborundum. These are cheaper than the full-grained grade. Both grades, however, will give many years of service if not ill-treated — such as being placed too near the fire so that natural oil in the skin is dried up. Cowhides and moroccos are a different proposition to piece materials to lay out and cut.

Planning out The size of a hide is calculated in square feet and includes all the inlets and peninsulas. In fact, looking at a hide laid on the floor it can be likened to a map. The measurements include all the coastline. One of the methods of measuring is by a Turner pin-wheel machine, which registers every inch of hide. There is bound to be a certain amount of unavoidable waste. When measuring a chair or settee for hide, note where inches can be saved, such as at the two edges of the inside back, where the arms merge into the back, also on the inside arms at this point. Plan the positions of these pieces on the hide, marking out lightly with ordinary chalk. Keep a good look-out for objectionable blemishes, such as small holes made by the weevil fly, abrasions caused by injuries to the animal when alive or during the skinning and dressing processes. Some blemishes are not objectionable and occasionally add to the natural effects of the skin. A careful examination in a good light is necessary, as often innocent-looking marks turn out nasty eyesores when the hide is stretched over a job.

Handling moroccos Avoid handling moroccos with damp or perspiring hands and carefully shade before cutting. There is often a slight variation in the shades of different skins. Another point to be noted when using morocco is that the markings along the backbone stand out fairly clear. These should be centred on the seats and backs, as when using a patterned material. All seams, borders, facings, etc., require a piped finish. This means accurate fittings on the actual job before cutting. Accurate fitting and cutting are vital if a clean finish is required, as leather cannot be manipulated like a soft cover and mistakes are not easily rectified.

Small joins and joins in obscure places can often be made by skiving one piece of hide to another. Lay one of the pieces to be joined on a flat board and with a very sharp knife make a long, slanting cut along the edge about to be joined. A thin knife well sharpened on an emery board makes a good clean cut. The other piece to be joined is cut on the reverse side to the first piece and the two pieces are glued together. Use a good flexible glue and after pressing together as tightly as possible wipe off any surplus glue. Lay aside on a flat surface until the glue is set. Short pieces of waste can be cut up for piping and made into one strip by this method. In fact, the old-time upholsterer used to join up quite large surfaces by skiving.

Occasionally one meets with a re-cover job of a different type. Rounded arms and backs, well-stuffed wings all mean that the hide or morocco must be neatly worked into pleats, or the fullness evenly spaced and distributed round a curved surface. Taking a scroll-shaped arm as an example, the hide is pulled over the scroll of the arm as tightly as possible and fixed temporarily in place on the underside. The spare material on the front of the facing is gradually worked into a number of evenly spaced folds. This is done by alternate straining and fixing with temporary tacks. Endeavour to keep the top surface clean of all rucks. If the folds are evenly distributed and tacked or sewn into place but not definitely pleated down flat, this usually makes a more pleasing finish. A thick piece of hide can sometimes be helped into place by damping the back, but don't overdo it so that it shows through on the surface.

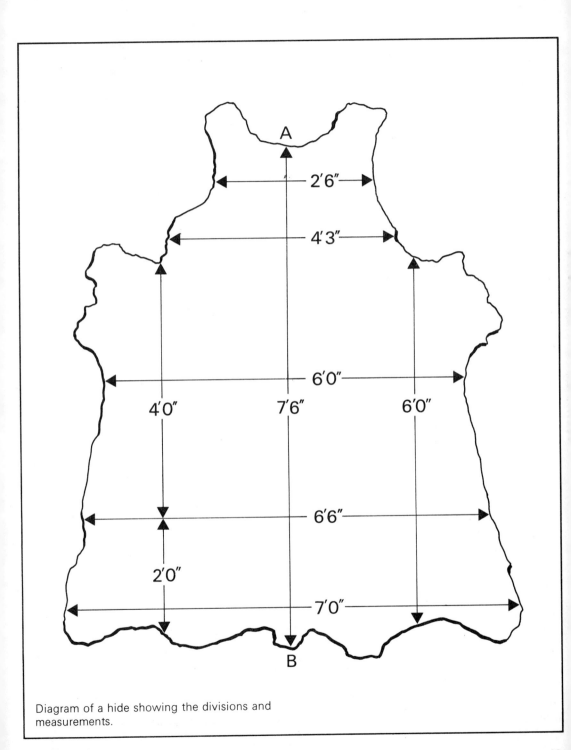

Diagram of a hide showing the divisions and measurements.

Rolls, facing, etc. The rolls and edges need to be cleaner and a little firmer for hide covering. Front borders are one of the places where accurate cutting is necessary, particularly when the piping is under the roll or edge. Another place is on the back round the arms. Clean out all fullness when fitting before marking and cutting to shape. Where fullness has to be retained, such as on the fronts of scroll-shaped arms and over the edges of wings, it should be neatly and evenly spaced out. Each case must be treated individually, but as previously mentioned fullness worked out evenly in loose folds rather than in hard pleats folded down tightly looks better.

Whenever possible covered wood facings on this type of work are a neat and efficient finishing method. Studs and banding are occasionally used, but antique round-headed nails spaced about 25mm. (1in.) apart and used both with and without banding are more in favour at present. Lead moulding, half-round in section with pins imbedded at intervals, covered with a piece of the morocco being used was one of the recognized finishes on good-class work. The two edges of the strip of morocco were sewn together at the back of the moulding. When carefully tapped into position the covered moulding formed a neat and dignified finish. Flexibead is an up-to-date finishing beading which has taken the place of the bead moulding. It is shown in Fig. 1.

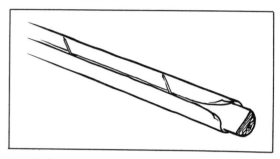

Fig. 1 Example of flexibead.

Chapter nine

Loose Seats and Other Small Seats

The ordinary dining-room chair having a loose drop-in seat, usually covered in leathercloth or hide, is familiar to most of us, Fig. 1. This method of fitting a seat has been in use for many years and is still popular. The loose seat, as its name implies, is made separately from the rest of the chair frame. This makes for a clean finish, no gimp, banding, or other trimmings being required. It can also be easily removed for cleaning and re-upholstering.

Fig. 2 shows alternative plans and sections of a seat. That to the left rests on the corner brackets. To the right the rails are rebated to hold the seat. In many modern chairs only the side rails are rebated as in Fig. 1. Birch or beech are the best woods to use for the frame, although quite a lot of the older frames were made of deal mortised and tenoned or halved together. Present-day practice is to use up any oddments of hardwood and dowel the joints, which is satisfactory if properly done.

Fitting the seat Before starting to upholster make sure the seat is a good fit. Test it to see that it is true and does not ride on the corners. Then, having decided on your covering material, see

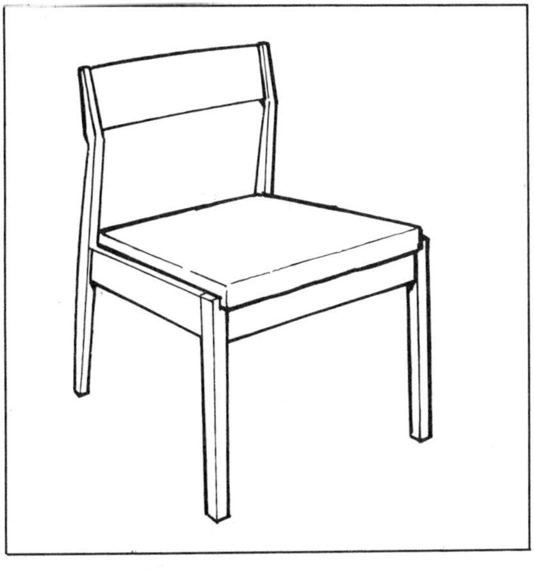

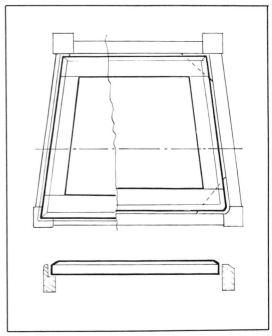

Fig. 1 Chair with loose seat.
Sometimes the chair rails are rebated but in any case there should be clearance all round. This varies with the material, but 3mm. ($\frac{1}{8}$in.) is about average.

Fig. 2 Alternative plans and sections of loose seat.

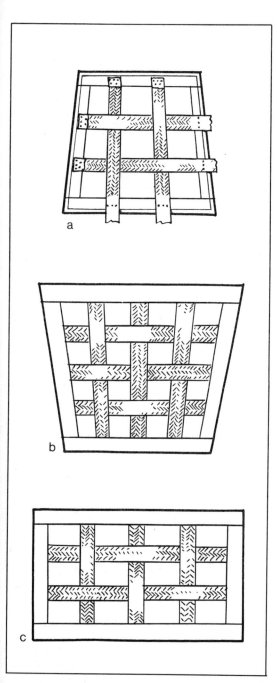

a

b

c

Fig. 3 Arrangement of webs on different shapes and sizes of seats.

that there is just sufficient space all round the seat frame to take the thickness of your cover. Too much space means an unsightly gap either all round or perhaps at one or two points only. This can be corrected by tacking a piece of cardboard along the loose side, or, if it is a very wide gap, a piece of web doubled or trebled over and tacked along will be better than the cardboard as it will give when placed in the chair.

Referring again to Fig. 2, note the position of the chamfer round the top. This should finish level with the top of the outside rails of the chair. If too high it results in an unsightly finish to the chair, and if too low it comes to the same thing, or involves a lot of trouble in getting the correct level with the stuffing.

Coming to the actual upholstering, hundreds, probably thousands, of these seats are turned out yearly by chair manufacturers, and all they consist of is the frame with a piece of plywood or fibre-board nailed on the top, and two thicknesses of linter's felt laid on and then covered. After being sat on a few times the linter's felt compresses and there is very little difference from sitting upon an ordinary wooden seat. Of course they do not wear out quickly, because there is nothing to wear, but the extra cost of webbing a seat is more than repaid by the comfort enjoyed.

Webbing Decide upon the number of webs according to the size of the seat. A modern dining-chair loose seat measures approximately 400mm. (16in.) by 350mm. (14in.) and two webs each way as shown in Fig. 3A are sufficient. A larger seat requires three each way, Fig. 3B, whilst a dressing-table stool or other long, narrow seat three and two, as in Fig. 3C. Tack the centre web first whenever there is an odd number of webs being used, and equalize the others between that and the frame. Start to web from back to front, tacking on the top of the back rail with five tacks, doubling over the web, and staggering the tacks as shown.

Place the edge of the doubled part of the web along the top line of the chamfer. The web must now be tightly strained to the front, and this will be found awkward, as the seat will lift up as soon as the webbing is stretched. Fix the seat to the bench with a G-cramp.

Fig. 4 Using the web strainer.

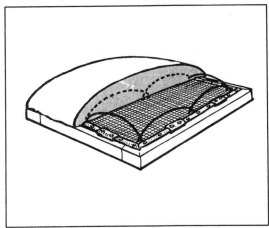

Fig. 5 Section through loose seat.
This shows the hessian tacked off, loops of twine and stuffing contour.

The method of using the bat type of web strainer is shown in Fig. 4. The web is doubled and passed through the opening. A bar either of wood or a piece of 12·5mm. (½in.) tubing is put through the loop of web and the bottom end of the strainer is placed on the edge of the rail with the return end of the web under it and levered down. Do this several times until you have got the knack of it and can get the web tight and in the correct place. Tack off with three or four tacks. A 15·6mm. (⅝in.) improved tack is usually the best size for all webbing, but if you have a light frame use 12·5mm. (½in.) improved tacks. Cut off the web about 25mm. (1in.) from the tacks, but do not turn over yet. Proceed with the other webs, checking the side ones under and over.

Hessian A piece of hessian is now required about the size of the seat over-all. Fold over about 12·5mm. (½in.) of one side of this and tack it along the top of the back rail with 9·4mm. (⅜in.) or 12·5mm. (½in.) improved tacks. Slightly strain to the front and fix with three temporary tacks. Repeat this operation at the side, keeping the threads of the hessian straight. When you have done this carry on with the tacking, stretching it as tightly as possible. Begin at the front centre and work all round, placing the tacks evenly. The raw edge can now be turned over, also the webbing raw edges with it, and tacked off.

Stuffing If you have undone an old seat you may find a little stitched edge around the front and the two sides and a piece of wood nailed on the back rail to form an edge. On another type of seat a roll of straw evenly stranded and covered with scrim is used. Should the shaping of the chair be such that you cannot do without these edges or rolls, they must be replaced or new ones made, but there are not many of these types of seats in use at the present day.

The usual method is to stuff the top with wool or hair. Hair is the best and amply repays the extra cost involved. Place a few loops of twine along the top edges of the seat, using a bent needle (half circular, spring, or packer's needle), just catching the edge of the hessian; also two loops across the centre. These are to prevent the stuffing from moving about and becoming irregular. Begin picking the hair or wool under the back loops and continue along the sides and front, finishing across the centre. Pick it out evenly, thin at the edges and coming to the thickest point on the crown of the seat, that is, slightly in front of the centre of the seat as in Fig. 5. The amount required varies according to the size of the seat and the quality of the stuffing; it should be firmly stuffed but not rammed in. An average seat takes rather less than 1lb. of hair.

It is advisable to cover with calico before the final covering, particularly if hair stuffed. Lay a tape measure fairly tightly over the stuffing and allow an inch all round. Cut this size of calico, and fix it with three temporary tacks along the back edge. Pull it over the stuffing, pressing down lightly, and fix at each corner of the front edge. Place a tack or two temporarily in between. Do the same along the sides, and, starting from one side again, repeat the process until a nice even contour has been obtained. Finally tack off the sides first, then the front, and lastly the back. Do not turn in but tack the raw edge and trim off with scissors or a knife just above the bottom edge of the frame.

Final cover The final cover can now be cut to size allowing 18·75mm. ($\frac{3}{4}$in.) to 25mm. (1in.) all round. If a patterned cover centre the main feature of the pattern to the middle of the seat. Place a piece of wadding over the calico if hair has been used otherwise the hair will come through. Place this wadding over the top of the seat only, allowing none to hang over the edge, otherwise the seat will not fit in the chair. First lay the cover over the seat in the correct position, then turn the seat and cover over together, and place three temporary tacks at the back and also three at the front to hold the cover in place.

Until this stage all the work has been done with the seat flat on the board or table, but now the easiest plan is to work with the seat on its edge, Fig. 6. As the cover is tacked off on the underside place two or three fixing tacks along each side, straining the cover slightly as you proceed. After the cover is fixed on all sides start the final tacking off along one side about 50mm. (2in.) from the front corner, and finish about the same from the back corner. Repeat along the other side, straining the cover slightly and helping it with a smoothing movement of the left hand. Proceed in the same manner with the front, then the back, leaving the corners until last.

When tacking off watch the cover to see that the pattern remains central and the threads of the material square. P.V.C. fabrics and hide have no pattern to worry about, but it is advisable to keep the material square. Remember also to keep an even strain on the cover from tack to tack so as to avoid ugly 'cat's teeth', as they are termed—that is, a little dip at each tack.

Fig. 6 Working position when covering.
If held on edge it is easy to smooth out the cover and tack beneath.

At the corner it is easiest to make a double pleat, as this lessens the amount of material to get away at each side. Pull the centre point of the cover over tightly and tack. Fold one side of the remaining material and pull down as tightly and cleanly as possible. On all excepting the thinnest of covers it is best to cut a V-shaped piece out, as shown in Fig. 7, but do not do this until you have formed the pleat, tried it once or twice, and are quite sure of the position. Some loosely woven materials will pull out almost without pleats at all and the cheaper P.V.C. fabrics are easy to work, but in the case of a very heavy material it is sometimes advisable to chamfer a little piece off the seat-frame before starting to upholster. With the majority of covers, though, due care and a tap with the hammer to flatten will make a clean finish and a good fit.

When all the tacking off is finished trim off the waste cleanly. Hide or leathercloth is best done with a sharp knife and, providing it is cleanly and evenly done, no bottom covering is necessary. Tapestry, moquette, and other soft covers require a bottom cover to present a neat finish. Black linen, black hessian, calico, or hessian are the usual materials used for bottoms. Tack on neatly, turning the edges under and spacing the tacks evenly.

The pincushion seat Before leaving the subject of the smaller types of seats it is advisable to mention the pincushion seat, Fig. 8. The whole treatment except that of the final cover is the same as for a loose seat, only all the work is done on the chair itself. There are one or two points which must be watched. There is usually only a narrow piece of frame left for the upholsterer to tack all his materials upon, so care must be taken when tacking that the wood is not split too much. Use fine tacks with all materials and rest the frame on something solid when driving the larger sizes home. If working on a polished frame place a piece of material under the web strainer to prevent scratching. The raw edges must be turned in.

A bottom is not required on this type of seat, but a finishing trimming is necessary to cover the tacks around the edges. On a soft cover this can be a gimp or a braid, though with leathercloth and hide a banding is customary. The banding can be tacked on either with studs to match, or brass nails spaced evenly.

Some types of pincushion seat chairs look very well if the cover is finished 'close nailed' with antique copper or brass nails. For this tack off the cover first with 9·4mm. ($\frac{3}{8}$in.) gimp pins instead of tacks. This saves quite a lot of angry words as you will often find a tack head where you want to place a nail.

The secret of success with all the smaller types of seat having no springs and only one layer of stuffing is to use best English black and white web for the foundation and hair for stuffing. The fore-

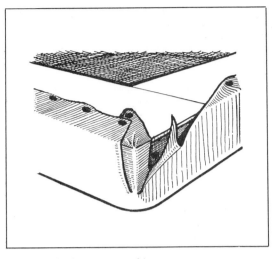

Fig. 7 Finishing corner of loose seat. The corner is drawn right over and a pleat formed at each side.

going remarks apply to the use of traditional materials and methods. On all the cheaper grades of loose seated chairs, 4mm.-ply or hardboard are nearly always used in combination with poly-foam, usually 25mm. (1in.) thick. This can also be used on a webbed seat preferably a little thicker or of a firmer grade. Foam is much easier to use than the older fillings, and it gives a resilient 'feel' for a fairly long period according to quality. Of course 25mm. (1in.) thickness on a piece of ply on a dining chair seat doesn't give a very soft seat, but one rarely sits on a dining chair for very long.

Chapter ten

Stools,
Slipper Box

The sizes of stools vary considerably, the ordinary fireside type being about 425mm. by 275mm., height 300mm. (17 in. by 11in., height 12in.). A much larger member of the family is called a fender stool. It is about the same width and height, but much longer, usually ·9m. to ·95m. (3ft. to 3ft. 2in.) over-all. Then there is the altogether higher stool for occasional use or for use with the dressing table.

Fireside Stool

Choose a type of leg which will match the furniture with which it is going to be used. The Jacobean twist in Fig. 1 looks well with hide or leathercloth covering. Having decided upon the size, prepare the seat rails. Birch or beech is suitable for the top seat rails, and these should finish 43·7mm. by 28mm. (1¾in. by 1⅛in.) If the style of leg requires an underframe keep this as light as possible, about 28mm. by 18·75mm. (1⅛in. by ¾in.) being quite heavy enough. It is advisable to mortise and tenon all joints. Glue and cramp, allowing the glue to set before fitting corner braces. Fix with glue and screws. When the frame is completed clean up with glasspaper and stain to the desired shade.

Webbing Begin by stretching two webs each way across the top of the seat. Tack the webs on the rails with 12·5mm. (½in.) improved or ⅝in. fine tacks. Fix the longest way first, doubling over the web when tacking on. Strain over tightly and tack off the raw edge, leaving an inch of web to be turned over later when the hessian has been fixed. Check the cross webs under and over, and strain and fix in the same way.

Place a piece of hessian over the webs, tacking this on with ¾in. improved tacks, turning over the edges all round, not omitting the ends of web. A thin roll about the size of the little finger is made around the edges. Cut a 50mm. (2in.) strip of hessian and tack this on to the top of the frame close to the outer edges. Put a little fibre on to this strip, then turn the hessian over and tack down so that a small roll or edge is formed all round. Make about six loops of twine around the top 50mm. (2in.) inwards from the edge, Fig. 4.

Left: A useful cushioned-top stool in *Dralon* finished with a ruched edge and a fringe. *Maples Ltd.*

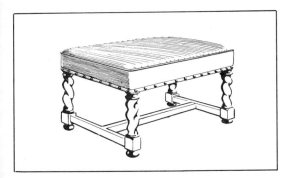

Fig. 1 The Jacobean style stool
This has a light underframing of 37·5mm. (1½in.) by 18·7mm. (¾in.) stuff. The seat rails, however, are heavier, being 43·7mm. (1¾in.) by 37·5mm. (1½in.).

Fig. 2 Stool of the eighteenth century. This could be made in either mahogany or walnut. Note the attractive finish given by the piped border.

Stuffing A thin stuffing of wool, fibre, or hair is picked evenly under the twines. Cover this with a piece of calico, fixing on each side first with temporary tacks. Pull down and tack off evenly on the outside edges of the seat rails with ⅜in. fine tacks.

Cover The next process is the final covering, finishing with a piped border around the edge. Cut a piece of cover 12·5mm. (½in.) larger all round than the top, then four pieces for the borders. Lay the centre piece on the top of the seat and fix with a few skewers or large pins along the top edge of the roll. Trim this piece off to within 9·4mm. (⅜in.) of the pins, then fit the borders around the edges in the same manner and trim off. Make a few notches around the edges before removing both borders and centre piece from the stool. These notches are made for guidance when machining together.

A piece of piping long enough to go round the top is made up, and the centre piece and borders are machined together with the piping between. Stitch a plain seam without piping at each corner.

This method of making a piped border can be used with either a soft covering material or hide and leathercloth. Place a piece of 12·5mm. (½in.) foam over the calico before laying the cover upon the seat. Temporarily tack the cover along each side until it is evenly strained all over, finally tacking off on the underside of the seat rail, turning in and spacing the tacks evenly. Tack around the legs at each corner raw edge, and trim off with a sharp knife.

Finish with a gimp on soft covers, studs, or antique

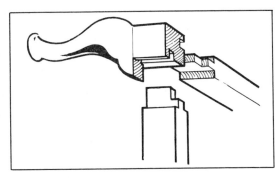

Fig. 3 Frame joints.

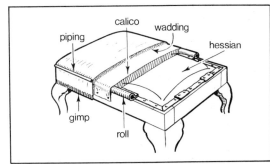

Fig. 4 Method of upholstering.

nails and banding on hide, etc. The gimp can very often be glued or pasted where a thin material is used. Otherwise use 9·4mm. ($\frac{3}{8}$in.) gimp pins and hide the heads under the scrolls of the gimp. It is advisable to complete the polishing of the legs before gimping.

Alternatively use a piece of ply on the seat. Obtain a piece of 50mm. (2in.) foam and cut to fit the seat, plus 6·25mm. ($\frac{1}{4}$in.) all round. Attach the foam to the seat by using a piece of adhesive tape fixed all round the foam. Pull it down to the seat top and tack the loose·edge of the tape to the side of the frame.

A pleasant effect can be obtained by using a piece of needlework for the top and a face cloth, or velvet, for the borders. Lay the centre piece of cover on the top of the foam and pin it in position with skewers. Cut around it to fit, also cutting the borders to fit, plus a 25mm. (1in.) sewing allowance extra for tacking off. A sewing allowance of 9·4mm. ($\frac{3}{8}$in.) to 12·5mm. ($\frac{1}{2}$in.) all round is usual. Make up a piece of piping and machine it round the centre cover first. Join the border pieces together, then join them to the top. Lay a piece of linterfelt over the top of the foam, or better still, a piece of skin wadding. The seams will bed into this better than directly on to the foam.

Dressing-Table Stool

A stool of this kind, Fig. 6, is useful in both bedroom and living-room.

Fig. 6 Suitable for bedroom or living-room. Note the attractive finish given at the edges. Height is 335mm. (17in.) to the framework. Seat size is 360mm. (18in.) by 300mm. (12in.). For the living-room the height could be cut down somewhat.

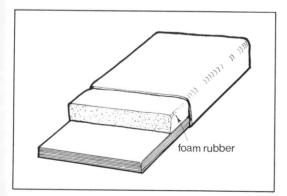

foam rubber

Fig. 5 Plywood seat covered with foam rubber.

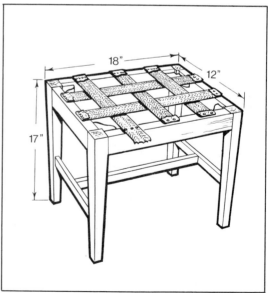

Fig. 7 Framework sizes and webbing details.

Framework The legs should be in good hardwood. They are tapered from 31·25mm. (1¼in.) square at the top to 25mm. (1in.) or 22mm. (⅞in.) at the bottom. Any odd pieces of hardwood can be utilized for the side rails. They finish 47mm. (1⅞in.) by 25mm. (1in.) and are tenoned into the legs. The two end stretcher rails are tenoned to the legs and the centre stretcher rail dovetailed from the underside. Glue and cramp up and fit blocks or braces in the corners. These are necessary for strength and should be well fitted before gluing and screwing. Fig. 7 shows the frame.

If this is to be upholstered in the conventional way the methods shown in Figs. 7 and 8 are followed. Webbing is the first item and it is advisable to use 12·5mm. (½in.) clout nails for this. Tacks, especially the 15·6mm (⅝in.) improved variety usually used for webbing, are liable to split narrow rails. Strain the webs on tightly, the short ones first, and check the long ones under and over as in Fig. 7. Cut a piece of hessian the required size, that is about 25mm. (1in.) larger all round than the top of the stool. Strain this on tightly, doubling over the raw edges and using 9·4mm. (⅜in.) or 12·5mm (½in.) improved tacks. A suitable cover could be a Boucle wool moquette or a nylon velvet. Both of these would make an attractive finish. More so if the piping was omitted and a matching ruche substituted. This would be machined to the centre cover in the same manner as the piping thus making a more dressy finish.

An alternative is to use the frame as a utility stool, finished with a buttoned seat covered in a P.V.C. coated fabric. Make the frame 25mm. (1in.) higher and use a heavy density foam 50mm. (2in.) deep. A more modern system is to make a separate frame and fix turned tapered legs as in Fig. 9. The ply-covered frame is shown in Fig. 10. For the ply base six 6·25mm. (¼in.) holes will be needed to take the button ties. A suggested mark-out for the buttons could be six buttons spaced at 100mm. (4in.) from the outside edges, and 150mm. (6in.) apart. The foam could be fixed to the base with an adhesive and marked out the same as the ply with small incisions at each mark. The cover is also marked out for the buttons. It is suggested the buttons should be square marked 150mm. (6in.) apart, and the pleats stitched in. This means an allowance for seaming, but if a stretch back P.V.C. is used no fullness allowance for buttoning is

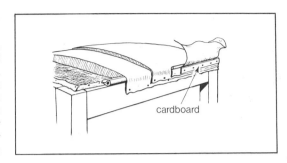

Fig. 8 How edging is formed. It is back-tacked.

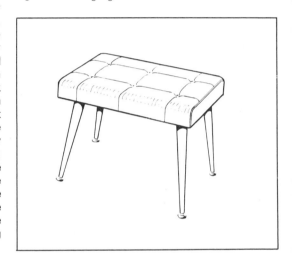

Fig. 9 Modern treatment for the stool with turned peg legs.

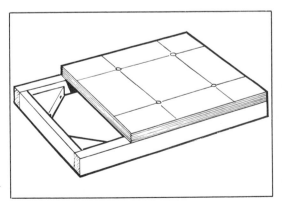

Fig. 10 Framework for the stool in Fig. 9.

needed. Mark out at 156·25mm. (6¼in.) apart from button to button each way. If the foam is cut about 6·25mm (¼in.) wider all round it will allow for a small amount of pulling inwards when being covered. Fold the cover over and crease across the pleat marks. The sewing allowance would be 6·25mm. (¼in.) each pleat. Machine the pleats across each way, taking up 3·12mm. (⅛in.) from the fold to the stitch. Before machining the borders and piping to the centre piece fit this piece over the foam and check that it is correct. The buttons, when fixed down tight should only take up the cover stretch in most of these fabrics, but if there is little stretch in the fabric allow more round the edges.

After sewing fit the cover over the foam and loosely fix with temporary tacks. Cut off six pieces of 6·25mm. (¼in.) dowel 25mm. (1in.) long or similar wood. Start buttoning with a double end needle and twine, pushing the needle through the hole in the ply to the corresponding mark on the cover. Return the needle to the same hole after picking up a button on the twine. Make a slip knot on the twine and pull towards the hole, and insert the piece of dowel, pulling tight enough to stop the dowel from slipping out. Continue with all the buttons, then clean out the cover all round and temporarily fix on the underside of the side rails. Make sure the cover is all clean and free from creases. Tack off, turning under to give a clean finish. Finally pull down the buttons and tie off with a knot on the twine above the slip knot, before cutting off the spare twine.

Slipper Box

This is a useful article, Fig. 11, serving the dual purposes of an extra seat and a hiding-place for slippers, magazines, etc. It can be made to practically any reasonable size in length and breadth, but the height from the floor should not exceed 350mm. (14in.).

The box Take as an example the following dimensions, 475mm. by 350mm. (19in. by 14in.) wide, total height over all 300mm. (12in.) The first item is to make the box, using 18·75mm. (¾in.) deal 200mm. (8in.) wide for the sides, and a piece of 6·25mm. or 9·4mm. (¼in. or ⅜in.) ply for the bottom. Dovetail the sides and ends together, and screw the bottom on temporarily. Also make four small feet and fix these to the bottom by screwing through the ply into the feet.

The lid is a frame of 50mm. by 25mm. (2in. by 1in.) hardwood with a piece of 4mm. plywood for the panel. Tenon the frame together, rebating the inside edges to take the plywood. Hinge the lid to the box. Make sure the lid fits flush all round, then remove it from the box; also the bottom.

Lining Line the inside of the carcase with a lining or casement cloth. Begin at the bottom edge of one side, strain to the top, tacking on the edge again. Leave about 18·75mm. (¾in.) over at each corner tacking at the top and bottom on to the edges of the

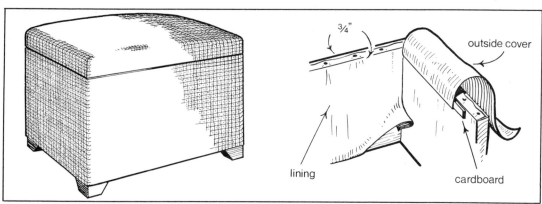

Fig. 11 Useful slipper box.

Fig. 12 Lining the box.
Note how the outside cover is back-tacked.

ends of the carcase. Repeat this procedure at the other side, then the two ends. When finishing the ends at the corners, fold 18·75mm. (¾in.) under and strain extra tightly to the top and bottom, creasing with the fingers whilst doing so. Cut a piece of the lining the size of the bottom and stretch this fairly tightly over the bottom opening, again tacking on the edges of the carcase. Next screw the ply bottom on over the lining.

Covering Covering the outside is carried out in like manner. Back-tack the cover at the top on to the inside of the box about 12·5mm. (½in.) down, as in Fig. 12. Stretch to the bottom and tack off on the underneath, neatly turning in and keeping the tacks evenly spaced. Tack the sides around the corners on to the ends before covering the ends. Treat these the same as the sides, folding inwards and creasing at the corners. If using a soft cover the corners can be stitched, but with P.V.C. material it is rather awkward. The side and end pieces can be cut to size and sewn, then drawn over the box. In this case the top edges cannot be back-tacked, but should be neatly gimp-pinned. Alternatively, the corners can be finished with antique nails spaced about 25mm. (1in.) apart.

Treatment of lid Tack a few loops of twine on the top about 37·5mm. (1½in.) from the edge all round, as in Fig. 13. Pick an even amount of fibre under the loops, and fill in the centre to a thickness of approximately 2in. Cover the stuffing with a piece of scrim, tacking it temporarily all round. Tack off finally on the top edge of the lid, making the finished height from the underside of lid to the top of the scrim about 62·5mm. (2½in.). Stitch a roll all round, using a sink or blind stitch first and a large roll stitch next. Keep the edge of the roll level with the edge of the frame all round as shown in Fig. 13. Second, stuff with a little wool on the top of the scrim and proceed with the covering. Lay this over similarly to the scrim, temporarily tacking first. There are two methods of finishing the covering. One is to tack off the raw edge on the underside of the lid, and in this case the underside must be covered with a piece of the lining neatly fixed with gimp pins. The other method is to finish on the outside edges of the lid, doubling under when tacking off. Cover these tacks with a banding and antique nails or a gimp. With this method it is necessary to stain and polish the inside of the lid. A double pleat is the best finish for the corners.

Replace the hinges and fit a short length of light chain to the inside of one end and to the underside of the lid to stay the lid when opened, see Fig. 14. Finish off by staining and polishing the feet.

A final tip, when back-tacking: place a 12·5mm. (½in.) strip of cardboard on the cover and tack through this so that the tacks do not cut the cover when it is turned over. Also it is much easier to keep an even line by this method, see Fig. 12.

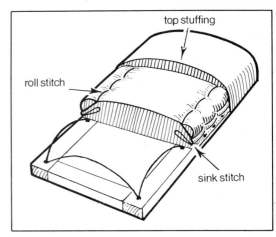

Fig. 13 Upholstering the lid.
The roll at the edge is essential to a good shape and durable seat.

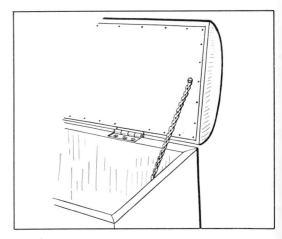

Fig. 14 How the lid is hinged.
A chain is desirable as considerable strain is otherwise thrown on the hinges.

Chapter eleven

The Fireside Easy

The term *Fireside Easy* is given to many different sizes and designs of the lighter type of chair as opposed to the fully 'stuffover' easy. Arms can be of various shapes of polished timber or partly polished and fitted with small upholstered pads on the top of the arm. A further refinement is to cover in the space between the underside of the top arm and the seat rail to keep out the draughts.

The shape of the back can be square as shown in Fig. 1 on the top rail, curved upwards or bowed outwards. Alternatively it can be serpentine or fitted with mock wings. Many pleasing and comfortable shapes can be made.

With the majority of upholstered frames, birch or beech are the woods commonly used, as they are cheap, make good dowelled joints, and also stain well to most of the popular colours. If a better job is required use birch for the covered parts of the chair, and oak, mahogany, or walnut for the arms and front legs. The sizes in Fig. 2 may be varied a little, but bear in mind the general proportions.

Framework Dowelling is the usual trade method with most joints on upholstered chair frames and is quite effective when carefully done, but, of course, a mortise-and-tenon joint can be used if preferred. Make a template of ply or cardboard for the back uprights and draw out a full-size plan of the seat. Mark out carefully the seat rails, noting the angles of the side rails. Cut off all these rails and the top back rail, and prepare for jointing. Also rebate the side seat rails 9·4mm. (⅜in.) deep and 12·5mm. (½in.) wide on the inside to take the spring fixings.

Assemble the back framework first. Glue and cramp up firmly. Follow with the front seat rail and the front legs and allow the glue to set before joining the back framing to the front. Two cramps are an advantage when putting the side rails in.

Now cut two further templates for the arm pieces, shaping them as in Fig. 2. Prepare and cut the arms, fitting them carefully before finally fixing. The two sides can be assembled independently and the front and back rails added after the glue has set. Note that the back frame is made up as a complete unit first.

Leave the frame until the glue is properly set and

Fig. 1 Concorde
Can be made up either as a loose cushion back or a tight covered back.

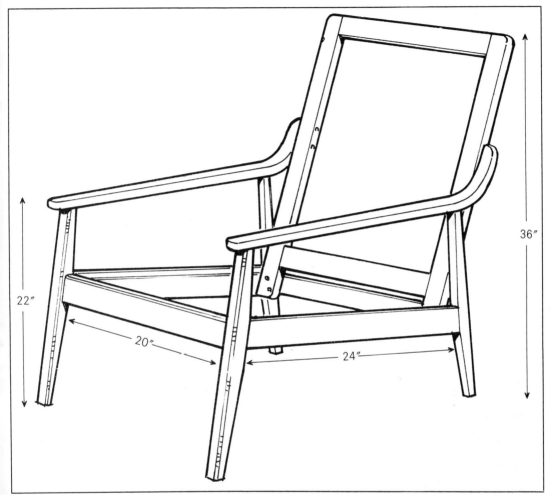

Fig. 2 Framework for Concorde.

then clean up the arms and legs with glasspaper before staining to the desired shade. You may now polish up to the final rubber if you wish, or leave the polishing until the upholstering is finished. In any case it is advisable to leave the finishing rubber until everything is done so that any scratches can be dealt with.

There are several ways of upholstering this type of frame. Starting with the back this can be sprung with 9·4mm. ($\frac{3}{8}$in.) tension springs stretched horizontally across the back framing. Six or seven evenly spaced springs fixed with staples on the front of the back uprights can be used. Two 12·5mm. ($\frac{1}{2}$in.) heavier gauge springs are advisable below the arms' level to give a firmer back support if so desired.

Cover the springs with either hessian or a fibre on hessian pad loosely tacked on all round. A certain amount of fullness must be allowed on the hessian to allow it to follow the springs when the weight of a person's back is placed against them. The stuffing or filling over the hessian can be a piece of 25mm. (1in.) or preferably 37·5mm. (1$\frac{1}{2}$in.) poly foam. Another method is to use a piece of rubberized hair covered with a good layer of linter's felt on the hessian. If the fibre pad is used it can be covered with an inch thick poly foam or a good layer of linter's felt. In most cases when using a fibre pad a little extra loose fibre or hair in the centre of the back helps to form a better back both for comfort and durability.

Covering The covering of the back is simple. Measure over the filling from the bottom back seat rail to the back of the top back rail. Also the width over the back from the back of each upright. Most covers are 1·25mm. (50in.) (approx.) wide so the inside and outside backs should quite easily be cut from the width. When patterned covers were more in favour it was usual to mark the centre of each piece of cover with a notch at the top and bottom. By making a centre mark on the top and bottom rails and meeting this with the cover it ensured the pattern was centered. It is quite a good idea to conform to this practice with all types of cover, as it saves time by ensuring the cover is squarely set.

Fix the cover on the bottom tacking rail with three temporary tacks and pull up to the top rail drawing the cover over to fix it on the back again with temporary tacks.

Continue similarly at the sides except that these must be cut round the arms. Lay the sides of the cover over the filling for a few inches and mark the place you must cut. After carefully cutting, turn back the cover and temporarily fix in place. Repeat the cutting on the other side of the frame, smooth out and tack down. Three buttons spaced at 137·5mm. (5½in.) apart just below the arm level will help to give a swell to the bottom of the back. The buttons are tied in with mattress twine used in a double pointed needle. Push the needle through the hessian at the back to the cover and pick up a button. Return the needle to the hessian and tie off with a slip-knot. Tie all three off evenly and secure with a knot in the twine above the slip-knot before cutting off. With the back completed carry on with the seat.

Below: Teak-finished saddle set. An up-to-date production by *G-Plan.*

Seat and cushion Seats cannot vary much in shape but can be in various sizes. The outside rails can be polished wood or covered across the front rail and along the two side rails with the cover being used. Most seats consist of a cushion supported on tension springs or rubber webbing. Also there are preformed rubber bases available. On this type of seat the cushion unit should be either latex rubber foam or polyether foam of a firm density. At least 87·5mm. (3½in.) thick on the edges, preferably 100mm. (4in.). It can be domed to about 125mm. (5in.) at the centre. An alternative shape frequently used is the rounded bolster front unit termed a *bible* front by the old tradesmen. This is an advantage when using polyether foam as many people sit on the front edge of a chair. Polyether foam loses its shape sooner than latex rubber so the thicker front looks better longer.

There are several ways of finishing the cushion covers. They can be boxed bordered with piped edges, ruched edges or plain seamed. Most of the seats on this type of chair are straight sided. If a plain cover or reversible pattern is being used it can be wrapped round the unit, meeting at the centre of the back border. Cut the cover to the required size, lay it over the cushion unit pinning it with two or three skewers at the back border. Mark with small nicks the position of the cover at both ends of the front and back borders. Cut two side borders to fit at these nicks. Remove the cover from the cushion and machine the borders in place, inserting a piece of piping all round the border if desired. Likewise a ruche or finish with a plain seam.

The back opening must be left to insert the foam unit, closing it afterwards either with slip-stitching the two edges together or with a zip fastener. Machine this the full width of the back and for preference use a nylon zip. A nice ruche makes a highly decorative finish whilst piping gives a clean streamlined effect. Plain seaming has come to the fore because it is simple to sew and it does not show the 'rubbing' in use like a piped seam although this does not occur on side seams. All fabric manufacturers recommend covering foam cushions especially latex foam with a light calico or lining before placing in the final cover. Complete the covering of the chair by fitting the outside back. Cut this to the required size. Fix it in place on the top back rail, slightly below the top edge and back-tack into position. Stretch tautly down to the bottom back seat rail and tack in place there, neatly turning under the raw edge. The sides are turned in and preferably slip-stitched in place. Alternatively they can be gimp-pinned or stapled in place.

Chapter twelve

Open Arm Fireside Chair

Fig. 1 Comfortable chair which can have either loose or tight cushions.

During the past decade vast changes have taken place in many trades and upholstery is no exception. New materials have been introduced and new methods of utilizing them have entered into many sections of the furniture world. The older methods of using loose hair, fibre, and flock, picking them in place under ties of twine, have been largely replaced by bonded materials. There is still scope for the specialist craftsman making individual items, but the large mass market is chiefly supplied by factory units using mass production methods. Their work has been made easier by the use of felted stuffings, rubberized hair, and foams both natural and chemical. Rubber latex foam is the natural foam and still the better all round product. Polyether and Polyester foams are chemical products and the chemists have made great progress with them. They have revolutionized the trade especially in the mass market section.

There are many grades and qualities, in fact at the time of writing Dunlopillo alone produce many different grades, and there are other firms also producing large quantities. Rubberized hair, felted cotton linters, and felted flock are modernized versions of the older forms of loose stuffings. These all make speedier methods of building up upholstery.

The spring-interior cushion, once largely used in cheaper fireside chairs, has been almost completely replace by polyether foam cushions.

Polyether foam is manufactured in sheets and can be cut to many shapes and sizes. This lends itself to building up interesting designs, such as the chair illustrated which inclines to the Scandinavian tradition. The show-wood parts should be of teak, that is, the arm sections. In practice the shaped top arm is often the only real teak piece, the remainder being beech or birch coloured to a teak finish. Another combination may be teak front upright or uphead, teak top arm, and the rest beech or birch. The covered parts are all beech.

Framework Teak is not the easiest of timbers to fashion but when nicely cleaned up with scraper, finely sanded, and oiled with a teak oil it both feels good to the touch and looks good. Assemble the arms first, mortising and tenoning the front and back up heads; also the seat side rail. A single 12·5mm. ($\frac{1}{2}$in.) or 15·6mm. ($\frac{5}{8}$in.) short dowel can be used on the top of the up heads to take the top

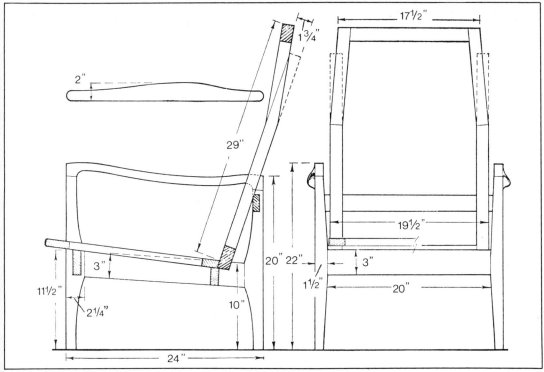

Fig. 2 Framework and measurements for Fig. 1.

arm rail. Use a good glue and cramp tightly, taking care that the glue is a non-staining type. When the arm frames have set join together with the front seat supporting rail, the back rail, and the back support rail. Use three dowels in each of the seat rails, and two in the back rail. Fig. 2 gives the main sizes.

Seat and back framing, Fig. 3, can be made up separately using birch or beech. Two 9·4mm. (⅜in.) dowels are advisable for the back joints and three on the seat frame. These frames can be upholstered separately and screwed in afterwards. The under-seat rail which supports both back and seat frames can be placed and adjusted before dowelling so it will give the desired pitch to the back.

Upholstery There are several ways of upholstering the frames. The seat can be tight covered or a loose cushion can be made up and the seat frame webbed and covered as a platform. The easiest

Fig. 3 Seat and back framing.

method for the back is a tight cover. It is suggested that Pirelli or similar rubber webbing and foam are used for upholstering both seat and back. Foamed latex rubber 87·5mm. (3½in.) deep is used on the seat, preferably slightly crowned. Take off the sharp edge of the inside edges of both seat and back frames with a rasp before starting to web. Tack three webs back to front on the seat frame and two crosswise. If possible use a small clout nail 12·5mm. (½in.) or 15·6mm. (⅝in.) in preference to a 15·6mm. (⅝in.) improved tack. Allow about 1 in 10 stretch on both seat and back using 50mm. (2in.) web on the seat and 25mm. (1in.) or 37·5mm. (1½mm.) on the back. Tack a piece of hessian over the webs on both back and seat loosely, making pleats around the edges to allow play when sat upon.

The foamed latex unit for the seat can be of the non-reversible type rounded at the two front corners. It should be fixed to the seat frame over the hessian. One method is to stick a tape around the bottom edge of the unit, either a piece of ready-made adhesive tape or ordinary wide tape with rubber adhesive. The lower edge of the tape is left about 12·5mm. (½in.) below the unit. This edge is tacked around the sides of the frame. Another method is to stick the unit onto the top of the frame with a rubber-based adhesive. Cover the whole seat and unit with light calico tacked on, raw edge on the underside of the frame close to the edge. A light, medium-density polyether foam is suggested for the back filling over about five 25mm. (1in.) wide rubber webs. This must be held in place similarly to the seat either with tape or adhesive, but calico is not needed over the polyether.

Covering The next item is the covering. Quite a number of covering fabrics can be used on a chair of this type. A fashionable choice would probably be a plain woollen weave to tone with the teak of the frame. Measure over the tops of the two units from the bottom of the back rails to the front edges of the units, plus 9·4mm. (⅜in.) on each. Cut these two pieces off and fit on to the unit tops to check, and round the corners, keeping the 9·4mm. (⅜in.) surplus all round for seaming. Cut off borders to fit round the front and two sides of both seat and back, allowing the 9·4mm. (⅜in.) for seaming and an extra inch on the back border for tacking on the back rails. Allow an extra 1½in. on the seat borders to turn under when tacking off.

Piped edges are avoided where possible over foam, as there is a tendency for the edges to roll out of place. A plain seam keeps in place better and does not show so much if it does move a little. After machining the borders on to the two top pieces fix them in place on their respective units. Temporarily tack the seat cover on to the underside of the frame, and the back cover also to the back of the back unit. Smooth out the covers and pull taut but not tight enough to lose shape.

When working with the older forms of stuffing the cover must always be pulled tight enough to pull down the stuffing to a certain extent. With foams this is not needed, but the cover must be taut without being pulled down to any great extent as otherwise the clean line may be lost.

Tack off the back cover on the outside of the back rail raw edge. The seat cover is tacked off on the underside of the rails and is turned in when tacking down thus making a neat finish to the underside of the seat. It will not require a hessian or black linen bottom. The two units can now be fixed in place between the arms meeting on the support rail. Screw through the support rail from the underside into the seat back rail. Screw the back to the seat where they meet on the support rail. Also screw through the back upright into the arms at the point of crossing. A 6·25mm. (¼in.) coach bolt or 14-gauge screw is needed.

The chair can now be completed with the outside back. This is back-tacked across the top back rail, stretched to the bottom rail, and fixed there with three or four temporary tacks. The side edges are turned in and temporarily fixed down the back uprights. Tack-off the bottom edge, finally on the underside of the seat support rail. Finish off the outside back by slip-stitching down the sides.

The neck or head pillow is just a small cushion made up of a light foam covered with the same fabric as the chair. It is held in place with a strap made of its own material. Fold a 125mm. (5in.) wide piece of material in half and turn in the two edges. Machine stitch along each edge, and insert a piece of elastic through the centre. It can then be slipped over the top of the back, making a comfortable neck rest. Join into the cushion-case midway as that is sewn together. This completes a chair that is comfortable in use and pleasing to look at.

Chapter thirteen

Fireside Chair

The chair in Fig. 1 was designed as a result of experiments in which height and slope of seat, pitch of back, slope of arms, and width were the chief considerations. The pitch of the back can in fact be varied after the main framework has been put together.

Latex cushions 100mm. (4in.) thick are used for both seat and back, and they are of the standard size of 550mm. by 525mm. (22in. by 21in.). They rest on Pirelli webbing, six strands for each. To enable the front edge to give when the chair is in use the front rail is curved at the top. Similarly the upper rail which supports the back is curved backwards so that the webbing can give.

If 50mm. (2in.) squares are obtained for the legs it will be found that they will easily finish to 43·75mm. or 47mm. (1¾in. or 1⅞in.) at the fullest part. Similar squares are used for the arms, these being shaped in both plan and elevation. The back legs are 25mm. (1in.) shorter than those at the front, and consequently the holes through the arms to receive the leg dowels have to be bored at a slight angle as in Fig. 2A. A full-size drawing reveals this angle. On the same drawing a plan of the leg with position of the seat rails can be given as in Fig. 2B. Although the rails are centred on the legs, the tenons are offset, the advantage being that they can be longer than would be otherwise possible.

Joints Since the rails meet the cylindrical part of the legs, flats must be cut on the legs to enable square shoulders to be sawn as in Fig. 2, although at the extreme top edges of the rails a hollow shape coinciding with that of the leg shape is cut. This serves to hide completely all traces of the mortice.

Obviously the two flats on each leg have to be at right angles with each other, and this calls for considerable care in hand work. Length marks are best made whilst the legs are still chucked in the lathe, and in fact it may prove convenient to do the actual cutting whilst the wood is still chucked, especially if the lathe has a dividing head which can be locked in the required position. A chisel can be used to cut away the bulk of the waste, but it is helpful to fix a strip of wood with parallel edges at the far side in line with the leg, and use a file to finish off, resting this on the wood as a guide. The second flat can be

Fig. 1 Comfortable chair with open arms and latex cushions for seat and back.

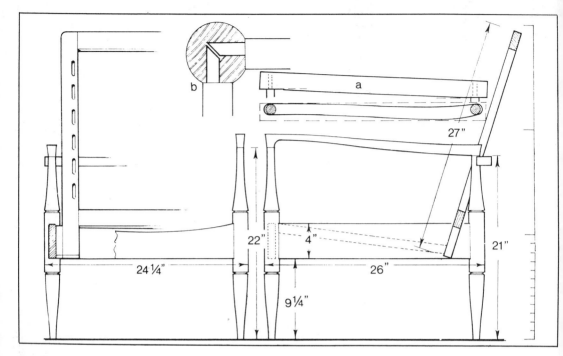

Fig. 2

cut similarly, care being taken to see that it is at right angles with the first.

Morticing On the flats gauge marks have to be put in to mark the mortices, and it is necessary to cramp a block of wood with parallel edges to one side to enable the mortice gauge to be used. Without this there would be no flat surface against which the gauge could bear.

Arms Since the squares from which they are cut slope downwards towards the back it is necessary to cut the underside at the ends at a slight angle so that the dowel shoulders of the legs make a close fit. At the front this entails cutting slightly into the underside, and sloping off the back as shown in Fig. 2A.

The arms are sawn to shape in both plan and elevation, and are roughly cleaned up, final trimming being done later. As the dowels pass right through and are wedged the holes are elongated at the top so that when wedges are inserted across the grain the dowels have a roughly oval shape.

Assembling The two dies are put together independently. First the seat rail is cramped, and the arm knocked down. It will be found that cramps can just be put on at the ends short of the dowels.

Once the wedges have been glued and driven in the cramps can be removed. When the glue has set the arms can be finally shaped and cleaned up, after which the front and back rails can be added. Corner braces can be screwed in when the glue has set—it may be necessary to cut away the back brackets later to enable the back to be added.

Back In width this has to fit between the side frames, and this necessitates gluing on block at the bottom so that the sides reach to the side rails, Fig. 3. Screws are then driven in from the inside into the rails.

Webbing In the chair in Fig. 1 the rubber webbing for the back is passed through slots in the uprights, Fig. 4, and held with screws or tacks driven in at the inner edges. At the seat, however, two notched strips are fixed with screws to the rails as in Fig. 4.

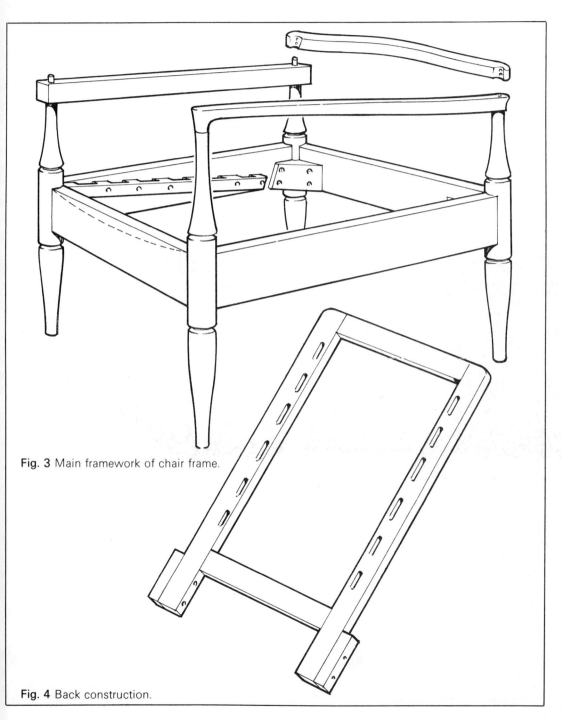

Fig. 3 Main framework of chair frame.

Fig. 4 Back construction.

The webbing is passed through the notch and fixed beneath the strip with tacks. It is drawn to the other side, passed through its notch, and again tacked.

To support the sloping back a curved rail is screwed to the back of the legs at the top. Half-round notches to fit over the legs are needed at the ends. Give for the webbing is ensured by curving the centre part backwards. A single brass screw driven through a screw cup at each side keeps the back in position.

Three-seater settee with buttoned cushions and saddle arms. *G Plan*

Chapter fourteen

T.V., Sewing, or Knitting Chair

This chair without arms is ideal for either watching or working. Quebec birch or a good beech are still the best timbers for upholstery frames, but may not be easy to obtain. If not available use close-grained timber that is unlikely to split.

Framework Mark out the rails, cut, and clean to size. The seat and back side rails are rounded on the top edges excepting the 87·5mm. (3½in.) left square on the rear end of the seat rails to take the back uprights. These latter two uprights can either be grooved or bored to take the tension springs. Boring separate sockets the diameter of the springs as in Fig. 2 is probably the neatest way of fixing the back springs. The seat springs are fixed to the back and front seat rails. Therefore these too must be either bored or grooved. Grooves are favoured here as they are practically unseen.

The side seat rails and back uprights are dowelled together using three dowels for each joint. As it will have to take a good deal of strain, cut the angle on the back uprights accurately, use a good glue and cramp hard to ensure a sound joint. Allow

Groove
for springs

18¼"

Fig. 2 Framework.
Note that the spring sockets in the back uprights are not taken right through.

Fig. 1 A comfortable chair on contemporary lines.

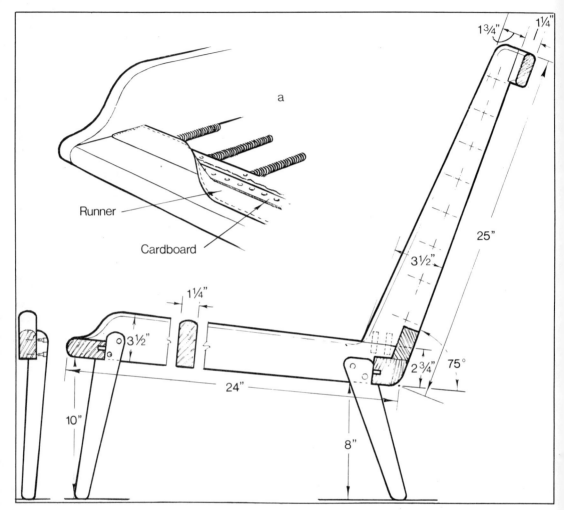

Fig. 3 Through section of frame, with main dimensions. Note that the legs are half-lapped to the side rails. The slight outward splay ensures that the weight is directly on the foot. Detail **A** shows the method of fixing the front seat runner.

ample time to thoroughly set. When these sections are ready they can be linked together with the cross rails, i.e., the seat back and front rails and back tacking rail. Leave the top back rail till last. This is a 37·5mm. (1½in.) bowed rail which is cut and lightly housed in the back uprights before gluing and screwing. The legs are cut to shape, cleaned, and half-lapped onto the side, front and back rails. When they are glued and screwed in position they also act as corner braces.

Polishing Well sand the visible parts before staining all over to shade required. Rub in some filler on the front edges and start the polishing. This can be by the older method of using button polish and building up first by brushing on, afterwards bodying up with a rubber. Rub down with a fine glasspaper between each application. If a spray

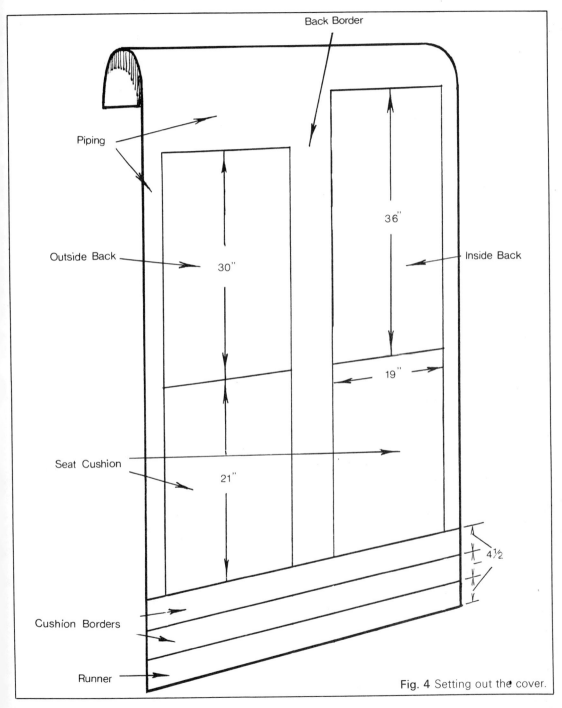

Back Border

Piping

Outside Back

30"

36"

Inside Back

19"

Seat Cushion

21"

4½

Cushion Borders

Runner

Fig. 4 Setting out the cover.

gun is available the whole of the frame can be sprayed and finished with a *pullover*. This method requires thin cellulose and a cellulose *pullover*. Alternatively a brushing cellulose could be used. This, too, is finished with a *pullover*.

A *pullover* is the trade name for a thin cellulose mixture used on a rubber. The rubber consists of a piece of wadding or cotton linters covered with a piece of clean washed rag. It is used both with french polish or with pullover. The wadding is soaked on its top surface with polish and the rag laid over so the polish works through the rag. In the case of french polish a finger-tip spot of neatsfoot oil is laid on the rag after it is pulled over the wadding. This lubricates the rubber and prevents it from sticking. The oil must *not* be used with a cellulose finish.

Before the polishing is completed, the back tension springs should be fixed so that any marks can be easily removed. It does not matter with the seat springs so much as they are nailed from the top of the rails and covered with material. Brassed or plated escutcheon pins are useful for fixing the springs as these are easier to remove should a spring require replacing.

Upholstery There is little complicated upholstery on this chair as a foamed latex cushion is suggested for the seat and a rubberized hair and linter's felt for the back, though foamed latex or poly foam can be used here also.

Eight 12·5mm. ($\frac{1}{2}$in.) diameter tension springs are needed for the seat and three for the back plus five 9·4mm. ($\frac{3}{8}$in.) springs. A first choice for the seat springs would be the braid-covered type and second choice the plastic-covered. It is doubtful if the 9·4mm. ($\frac{3}{8}$in.) size will be obainable in the covered type, but one of the larger-covered size can be used at the top and two at the bottom. As the back cushion is not reversible this does not matter except for appearance or if they rust.

The seat cushion is reversible so the seat springs must be covered either individually with braid or plastic, or an apron laid over them. The apron can be made of a lining or a thick fabric hemmed along the two ends and slotted at each side to take the first and eighth spring. The rest of the apron passes over the top of the other springs.

A piece of material 112·5mm. (4$\frac{1}{2}$in.) wide is cut from the covering fabric. Cut this the full width and divide into two 500mm. (1ft. 8in.) pieces, and make a small hem along one edge of each piece. These runners are stretched across the front and back seat rails and back-tacked to them so that the hems lie over the springs.

Cushions It is intended that a foamed latex cushion approximately 100mm. (4in.) at the edges and flat or only slightly domed should be used for the seat. The width should be 450mm. and 500mm. (18in. and 20in.) from front to back. It can be covered in almost any fabric and the small designs much in favour at the present time are suitable. Whether a large or small designed fabric is decided upon take the most prominent feature of the pattern for the centre motif. Make this the centre of both the seat and back cushions.

The back cushion can be made up with a piece of rubberised hair wrapped in one or two layers of linter's felt. If the linter's is a thick grade, one thickness will be enough as the cushion should finish approximately 62·5mm. (2$\frac{1}{2}$in.) thick at the centre. Add another layer of felt on the front at the top and bottom thus making a slight swelling at these points.

Most covering fabrics are 1·2–1·25m. (48 to 50in.) wide so the two panels for the seat cushion will cut from the width. This also applies to the front of the back cushion and the outside back. Cut these pieces only, leaving the strips in one length as these will be needed for the side borders of the back cushion. Allow 12·5mm. ($\frac{1}{2}$in.) for sewing all round for the panels. The seat cushion borders should be cut rather tight, approximately 112·5mm. (4$\frac{1}{2}$in.) to finish 93·75mm. (3$\frac{3}{4}$in.) on the piping. This will tighten up the cushion all round and give a clean finish. Cut the back cushion borders to the shape shown plus 12·5mm. ($\frac{1}{2}$in.) sewing allowance all round.

The back cushion is made up of a front panel, side borders, lining, and outside back. The front panel runs from the bottom of the side back borders, up and over the top of these to where it meets the first tension spring of the back. Here it is joined to the lining and the outside back.

A small hem is made on each side of the outside

back and across the bottom edge. Join the top edge of the outside back and the lining to the front panel first, then continue by joining the sides of the lining to the borders, thus making a bag of the front panel, the borders and lining, leaving the outside back loose on the sides and lower edge. Leave the bottom of the bag open to insert the felt-covered hair. When this is properly filled and evened out so there are no lumps or rucks the bottom is closed by slip-stitching.

Three buttons just below the top, and three above the bottom swellings will help to keep the shape of the cushion. Space the buttons about 125mm. (5in.) apart and tie in with a twine run through, using a mattress needle. Use either matching or contrasting buttons on the front but any odd buttons will suffice at the back as these are only to stop the twine pulling through when the slip-knot is pulled tight and knotted.

The back cushion rests on the back tension springs and is held in position by bringing the outside back over the top tension spring and down to the underside of the bottom seat rail. It can be tacked down here, but the cushion itself can be made easily removable by fitting four eyelets on the bottom hem of the outside back and four turn buckles on the bottom rail.

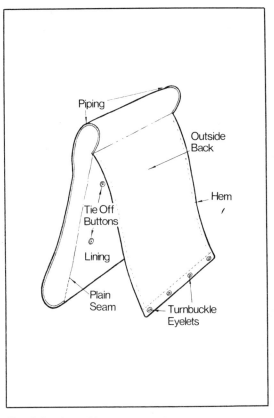

Fig. 5 Back cushion construction.

Cutting List

	Long			Wide		Thick	
	m./ft.		in.	mm./	in.	mm./	in.
2 Legs	·32	1	0½	50	2	31·25	1¼
2 Legs	·3	0	11½	50	2	31·25	1¼
2 Side pieces	·625	2	1	100	4	31·25	1¼
2 Back pieces ...	·6	2	0	100	4	31·25	1¼
1 Seat rail	·475	1	7		3	31·25	1¼
1 Ditto	·475	1	7	67·5	2½	50	1¼
1 Back rail	·531	1	9¼	67·5	2½	37·5	1½
1 Stretcher	·475	1	7	67·5	2½	31·25	1¼

Allowance had been made in lengths and widths. Thicknesses are net. In addition to the above are required eleven 12·5mm. (½in.) tension springs; five 9·4mm. (⅜in.) tension springs; foam rubber cushion 550mm. by 450mm. by 100mm. (20in. by 18in. by 4in.) rubberised hair and linter's felt; 1·8m. of 1·2m. or 1·25m. (2 yards of 48 or 50in.) material and 18·75mm. (¾ yard) lining.

Chapter fifteen

A New Form
of Comfort

During recent years quite a different type of easy chair has been growing up. The old style of office chair was often fitted with a simple swivel action.

A new type of swivel, or rock and swivel chair has evolved and is becoming an elaborate production.

It has been helped along by the moulded shapes of Polyurethane, Polystyrene and glass fibre 'shells'. The number of shapes, sizes and designs continues to multiply. Starting with the back and arms being tight-covered and a loose cushion in the seat, further developments have added cushions to the backs and, occasionally, on the arms. Methods of upholstery are fairly simple. The shell itself is covered with a layer of foam, generally on both the front and the back. Not less than an inch thick, polyether foam is needed on the inside arms and backs whilst about 9·4mm. ($\frac{3}{8}$in.) thickness on the outsides. The foam should be fixed with an adhesive all over to hold it in position. Most of the covers in use are of the knitted, stretch type which cling comfortably to the curves.

To a large extent, cutting the cover follows the principles of cutting a loose cover. In fact, many chairs are sold as loose cover designs, and spare covers can be obtained to replace or make a change whenever required. When making a number of units, it is usual to make a prototype and fit a cover to it. This can be removed and used as a pattern for any number required.

When making up a single chair or other unit, the first item is to measure each section of the unit, allowing sufficient for fitting and seaming before cutting. Pin the sections into place with skewers or large blanket pins, and pin together after cleaning out most of the fullness. Trim off and make a number of guiding notches around the cover before removing for sewing. If making a removable cover, allow enough material to make a fair size hem to take a cord or tape around the bottom of the outside arms and back.

Some designs may need an opening on the outside back or under arm to ease the cover into position. These can be closed with a zip fastener.

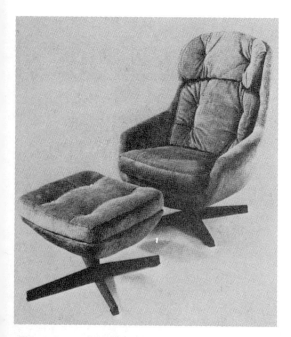

Fig. 1 A comfortable chair with deep-buttoned cushions and matching footstool upholstered in cotton corduroy. The chair rocks and revolves and the stool revolves. *Greaves and Thomas.*

Right: A suite from Greaves and Thomas with plain zip-on covers.

Fig. 2 Polystyrene foam shell. *Profile Expanded Plastics Ltd.*

Fig. 3 Profile of shell chair.

A tight cover can be cut to fit on the same lines and sewn whenever possible. If cushions are to be fitted to the back and seat, the inside back can be left open for two thirds down the centre of the back. The back, and the wings, if any, can be cleaned out and stapled down on the fitted splines; likewise, the bottom of the arms and seat platform.

On many shells, a piece of ply is needed on both the top and bottom of the seat moulding to strengthen it to take the swivel movements' fixings. The outside arms and back can be stapled to the ply on the underside, thus making a clean finish.

Early models of shells relied mainly on their contours for their comfort, but cushions have now taken over and are increasingly used. Two back cushions are shown on this chair, also the seat cushion. Their interiors can be various densities of foam, firm for the seat, soft or light for the back.

Foam covered with *Dacron* or similar materials make ideal cushions. They need a few buttons to keep their shape and also to keep them in position. For many years the upholsterer has aimed at cleaning out all fullness and creases as far as possible. This ideal has changed and the present trend is to have enough loose material to lightly crease and look soft. Therefore, after taking the cushion sizes or templates, do not cut too tight, allow for the buttons to sink in. The top back cushion will need to be fixed in place. Twine or fine wire ties can be made through the shell before fitting the covers, tying the buttons in when finishing off. The lower back cushion will usually lie in place between the seat and top cushion without fixing; otherwise, tie in on the top two buttons. Button the seat cushion through with four buttons top and bottom, tying off under the bottom buttons and tucking the cut ends of the twine under the buttons with the blunt end of the regulator, thus finishing with a reversible cushion.

Modern suite with pleated back and seat. *Lurashell*

Chapter sixteen

Period Wing Armchair

R. Tyzack Ltd.

Birch or beech is the most suitable wood for the frame, with walnut or mahogany for the front legs. Sizes and the general details are given in Fig. 2. A larger chair can be built up from these details, but the height of the seat and the arms from the floor should remain the same. The main seat joints require three or four 7·80mm. or 9·4mm. ($\frac{5}{16}$in. or $\frac{3}{8}$in.) dowels each, whilst two will be sufficient at the other joints. Braces glued and screwed into the seat corners will add to the rigidity of the frame. Before fitting the side seat rails rebate the inside top edges $\frac{3}{8}$in. deep and $\frac{1}{2}$in. wide for receiving the springs. After assembling the frame stain the legs and top, bottom, and inside edges or the seat rails.

Webbing Start by webbing the arms, one web across the centre of each arm and another about 1in. away from the back upright. Stretch on tightly and keep the end webs parallel with the uprights. Next tack a piece of hessian to the bottom tacking rail, strain to the top arm rail and tack off. At the end near the back upright fold the hessian over and sew it to the web with twine. Tack off the remaining end of the hessian on to the front upright. The back can be either of the firm type or sprung with tension springs. If the former, stretch webs from the bottom to the top and two crossways, spaced at equal distances and tacked on the front edges of the rails. The hessian is tacked on also from bottom to top, then along the sides, but do not strain too tightly sideways. If a spring back is desired fit seven cable springs equal distances apart, starting about 6in. from the seat rail. Fix these to the back uprights with staples or clout nails. Cover with hessian tacked on as for a firm back but with a certain amount of sag to allow for the movement of the springs.

Coming to the actual stuffing of the back there are several alternatives. Hairlok and fibre or hair woven on to hessian can be obtained cut to size and are simply tacked down at a few points to hold them in place. Otherwise a few loops of twine can be run across the hessian and loose fibre or hair picked under them. Start at the bottom with a thickness of about 3 inches graduating to nothing at the top. Cover with scrim and run through with a needle and twine, making long stitches and forming an oblong in the centre of the back. Another alternative is to use the fibre on hessian pad over the springs with an extra thick addition of fibre at the

Fig. 1 Wing armchair in period style. Although the main outline of the chair is on period lines, the upholstery is in the modern manner.

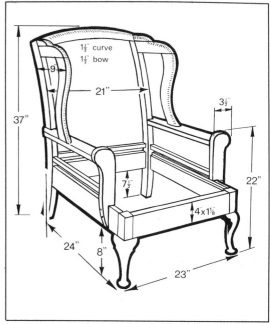

Fig. 2 Sizes and details of frame.

bottom. Before covering lay on a piece of foam 1in. thick. The space on the top of the arm rail also requires filling in with a little stuffing and covering with scrim.

Cutting the cover For the cover 3·3m. of 1·25m. (3⅔ yards of 50in.) material are required, this allowing for a reversible cushion. Take a rough template of the cushion size and carefully measure the other parts of the chair before cutting. The approximate sizes and a suggested scheme of cutting are shown in Fig. 3. This may have to be rearranged according to the pattern and material chosen. If the design has a prominent feature it should be centred on both the inside back and the seat cushion.

Cover the arms first. These require little stuffing; just a layer of linter's felt or a piece of foam. Tuck the cover through the opening between the arm tacking rail and the seat, and fix with temporary tacks. Pull the cover over the arm and fix it on to the

underside of the arm rail. Smooth out sideways and temporarily fix at the back and the front uprights. Make sure the cover is in the correct position then cut round the wing upright.

Finish off each arm and proceed with the back in a similar manner. The cover is tacked off on the front of the uprights and on the back of the top rail.

Covering the wings The wings are a little more awkward as the bottom edges of the cover are tacked on to the top of the arm rails, and the position must be carefully judged. The cover is tacked through the wrong side similarly to back-tacking, then laid over the arms whilst the wings are hessianed. Tack the hessian over the top of the cover on to the arms and on to the front of the wings. Do not fix to the back uprights until the covering is finished. A thin layer of hair covered with a thickness of linter's felt will be about the right quantity of stuffing, or an inch layer of foam over fibre or hair. Bring the cover over this stuffing

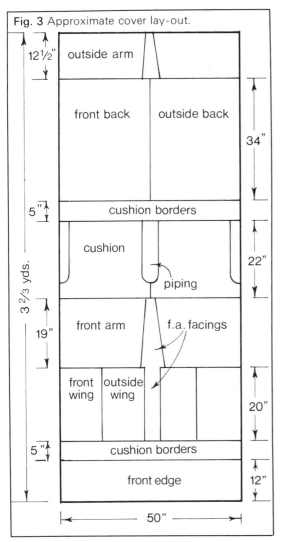

Fig. 3 Approximate cover lay-out.

outside arm — 12½"

front back | outside back

34"

cushion borders — 5"

cushion

piping

22"

3 ⅔ yds.

front arm | f.a. facings

19"

front wing | outside wing

20"

cushion borders — 5"

front edge

12"

50"

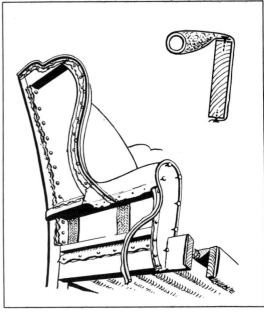

Fig. 4 Tacking off and finishing details. Inset is shown a section through the front seat rail and first cable spring.

Back-tack this latter piece of cover along the top edge of the front rail. Pass the loose edge under the first spring and bring it up between the first and second springs. Lay a piece of linter's felt between the first spring and the edge, afterwards pulling the cover over the front and tacking off on the underside of the front rail. This is shown inset in Fig. 4.

Make up some piping and tack pieces round the front facings, along the outside edges of the wings and across the top of the outside back. The outside wings, arms, back, and front facings are now tacked on in the order given. Temporarily tack where they make contact with the piping, afterwards sew with a half-circular needle.

The cushion can be either latex or plastic foam. A standard size of unit with two small pieces added to form the T-shaped front would be ideal. Check the template to fit the seat and cut the top, bottom, and borders, all with a sewing allowance. Make up the cushion case and insert the unit. Slip-stitch the back opening or use a zip fastener.

and fix on the outside edges of the wings. With a little careful manipulating the fullness can be worked out quite clean round the curved edges. When this has been done finally tack off. Also tack the back edges on the inside of the back uprights and finish the hessian here too.

Seat springing The seat tension springs can now be fixed in position, eight in all, spaced about 50mm. (2in.) apart. Cover the two small side pieces of seat rail before covering the front rail.

Chapter seventeen

Three-Piece Suite

This suite, Fig. 1 and Fig. 2 (see page 81), is built up by the traditional hand-sprung methods which have been used for many years in all parts of the world. They are still needed in top-grade bespoke work. Many current productions are designed for foam and patent sprung units. With some slight alterations of the tacking rails, sizes and positions, these materials can be used on this suite. However, a sound knowledge of the older methods will enable many awkward jobs to be tackled with confidence.

Chair The first item is the frame. Birch, beech, ash, maple, and oak in the order named are the choice of woods for preference. A close-grained hardwood capable of taking tacks without splitting and hold-ing dowelled joints is the ideal. After setting out and cutting to size the various rails, assemble the arm. Use good glue and cramp tightly. Join up with the seat and back rails, and fix the corner blocks with glue and screws. A 9·4mm. ($\frac{3}{8}$in.) hole is bored in the centre of each corner block to receive the castors. The last-named can be the detachable, generally called *push in* type. Fig. 4 shows the frame.

Webbing The frame completed, turn it upside-down, resting the seat rail on a trestle or bench corner, and start webbing. Six strands of good-quality web are required from front to back and five from side to side. Work from the front rail first, tacking on the web by folding over about an inch and using $\frac{5}{8}$in. improved tacks or clout nails. Space the strands about 43·7mm. (1$\frac{3}{4}$in.) apart, straining each one tightly with a web strainer. Tack down four $\frac{5}{8}$in. tacks through the single thickness of web, cutting off about 25mm. (1in.) beyond the tacks. Turn over this end and fix with two tacks. The side-to-side webs are alternately checked under and over the others. Having completed the webbing of the seat place the chair upright on trestles or bench. The arms are webbed next. Fig. 3 gives the general layout. Two webs are needed up and down on each inside arm; $\frac{1}{2}$in. improved tacks will be most suit-able for this webbing.

Springing Springing the seat is the next operation; six 10in. by 8 gauge, three 9in. by 9 gauge, and four 5in. by 10 gauge springs are required. The 9in. springs form the back row and the 10in. the middle and front rows. The position of the front

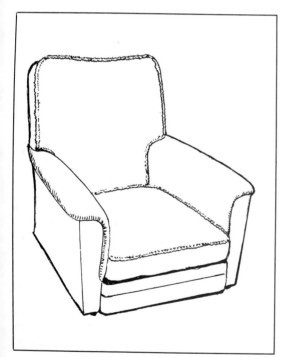

Fig. 1

Fig. 2 Comfortable fully upholstered settee. The armchair is shown in Fig. 1.

A soft cover is suggested for these items. Hide or leathercloth would be more difficult and would need a rather different build-up.

Below: Details and sizes of the chair frame and springing

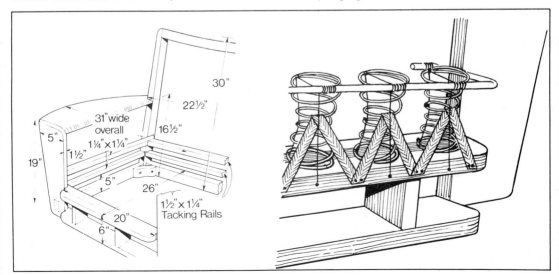

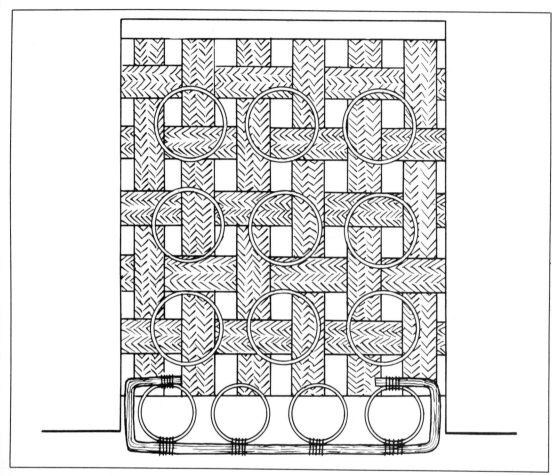

Fig. 3 Lay-out of springs and webbing.

row of springs is governed by the 5in. springs to be used on the front edge.

Hold one of the 5in. springs on the front rail and set the first row of 10in. springs about 25mm. (1in.) behind the top rung of this spring. The back row of 9in. springs is placed slightly in front of the back tacking rail, and the middle row is set midway between the front and back rows (see Fig. 3). Sew the springs to the web with three ties to each spring, the ties starting with a slip-knot and the twine kept taut between each tie. Tack a piece of hessian or odd soft material on the front rail as an anti-knock for the springs.

Lacing the tops of the springs in position with a stout non-stretch cord is the next item. Cut three pieces of laid cord, each to pass from the seat, back tacking rail, over the springs to the front rails, and returning to the top rung of the first spring; also allow for the ties. Fix a cord by tying round a tack on the seat tacking rail opposite each row of springs. Bring one of the cords to the second rung of a back spring, tie or half-hitch around the coil, and pass to the top rung. Carry on to the middle and front springs, tying on both sides of the top coil of the middle spring and one side of the top coil of the front spring. Bring the cord down to the second or third coil of the front spring. Pull taut

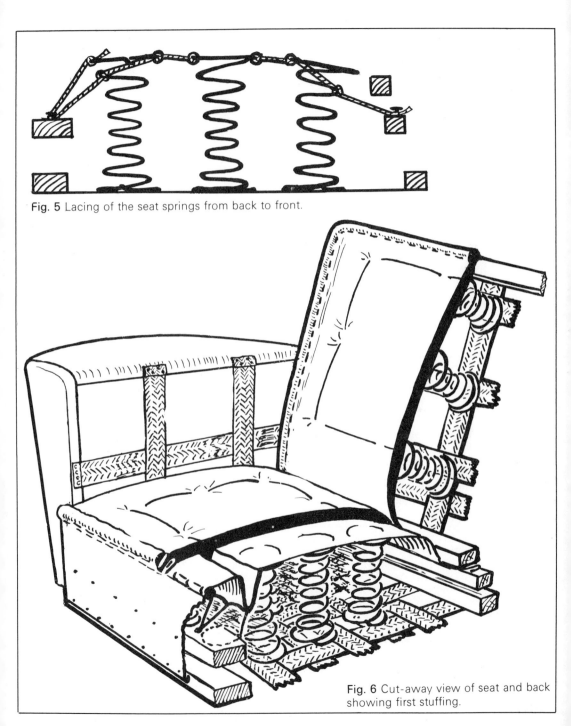

Fig. 5 Lacing of the seat springs from back to front.

Fig. 6 Cut-away view of seat and back showing first stuffing.

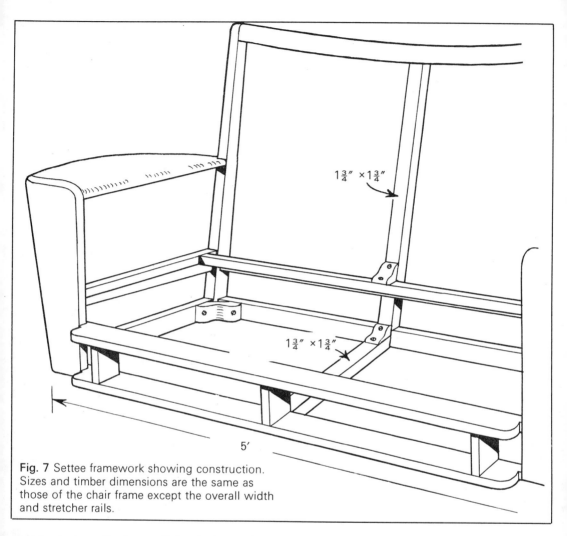

$1\frac{3}{4}'' \times 1\frac{3}{4}''$

$1\frac{3}{4}'' \times 1\frac{3}{4}''$

5'

Fig. 7 Settee framework showing construction. Sizes and timber dimensions are the same as those of the chair frame except the overall width and stretcher rails.

round a tack on the front rail, but before tacking make sure the springs are in their proper positions.

The back spring should lean a trifle outwards, the centre one very slightly forward and the front one rather more forward (see Fig. 5). When satisfied with the positions of the springs knock the tack home and return the surplus cord to the top rung of the front spring. Repeat over each row of springs from back to front, then from side to side.

Edge Springing The front edge springs are stapled to the front rail. Four in number, the two

end ones are about 18·75mm. (¾in.) from the arms, and the other two equally spaced. Cut a piece of web in half and tack one end on the front of the front rail. Pass the other end up and through a lower middle rung of the first spring, returning to the rail again and pulling the spring well forward before tacking down. Repeat with each spring. Next cut four pieces of laid cord long enough to pass from the rail over the spring and back to the rail. Tie one of these cords at the back of the bottom rung of a spring. Bring the cord to the middle rung and tie again, pulling the spring into an upright position. Carry on to the top rung and tie again, then to the second rung downwards, and so to the front edge of the spring rail. Repeat with each spring, tacking down the cords so that the top coils are approximately level with the front 10in. springs of the seat. The edge springs should finish upright in position.

The actual edge is formed by lashing a piece of cane or wire along the front edges of the top rungs of the edge springs. Use cane for preference about the thickness of the little finger. An 8-gauge wire or an old spring unwound and knocked out can be used. Bend each end round to form a return the size of the top coil of an edge spring. Lay the cane or wire on the edge springs and, using thin twine, whip the cane to the front edge of the top coil of each spring; also the returns to the back edge of the end springs. (See detail in Fig. 3).

The whole of the springing is covered with a heavy quality hessian. This hessian is tucked down between the front edge springs and the main springs to form a gutter or valley. Fix all round with temporary tacks except at the front. The gutter is held in place by a series of laid cord loops passing through the hessian and back to the front rail before being tacked down between the springs. The front portion of the spring hessian is brought over the springs and on to both front seat rails. Tack off the hessian all round with ⅜in. or ½in. improved tacks for preference. The tops of the springs are sewn to the hessian with three ties, using the same method as when sewing to the webs. The cane is also bound to the hessian with a series of half-hitches spaced about 37·5mm. (1½in.) apart. Finally, two loose loops of twine are made across the top of the front edge.

First stuffing in the seat These loops are to take the first stuffing, the next operation. Coco fibre (or *ginger* fibre, as it is commonly called) is most suitable unless horsehair is available. Pack a fairly firm, even amount along the sides and back of the seat and under the loops on the front edge. Fill the gutter firmly with hair or odd pieces of linter-felt. Also a thin layer of hair or fibre over the centre part of the seat just sufficient to avoid feeling the springs through.

Cover the stuffing with a piece of scrim or light hessian, securing it at the front with three or four skewers. Make a square of running-through ties in the centre of the seat, avoiding the gutter. Pick over

the front edge fibre and even out to form a compact firm edge. Refix the scrim in place with skewers, turning in the edge of the scrim. This edge is sewn to the hessian at the cane. A sink or blind stitch is also made across the front at this same point. Regulate the stuffing well forward with a regulator or stout needle.

Complete the edge with a top stitch to form a roll about the size of a thumb. Both kinds of stitches are started with slip-knots. Continue by inserting the needle about 37·5mm. (1½in.) ahead each time then returning it halfway behind the point of insertion. With the blind stitch the needle is returned before pulling clear of the scrim on the top of the edge. The twine is twisted round the needle as it is withdrawn and pulled taut. Turn in the edges of the scrim along the sides and back and tack down. This completes the seat for the present so the back can be dealt with next.

Back The webbing of the back consists of three webs up and down and four webs crosswise. All are tacked to the outer edges of the back uprights and rails with ⅝in. improved tacks. Six 6in. by 12-gauge springs are positioned on the crossing points of the top and middle webs and three 6in. by 10-gauge on the bottom two webs. They are sewn to the webs in the usual manner, but are not fully laced as in the seat. The top springs are pulled upwards by passing a piece of laid cord round the second or third rung of each spring and fixed with tacks to the top rail. The middle and bottom springs can be laced through their middle rungs from side to side. This will keep them in place whilst covering with hessian, which is the next operation. Tack down the hessian on the front edge of the rails, doubling over the edges. The tops of the springs are sewn to the hessian with three ties to each.

Make several loops of twine on the hessian about 50mm. (2in.) inwards from the side and top rails. Pick an even quantity of fibre under these twines and fill in the bottom and centre. Lay a piece of scrim or light hessian over the stuffing and fix in place with a few temporary tacks.

A square of running-through ties similar to the seat are made in the centre of the back. After running through, the scrim is tacked down all round. Aim at a fairly firm, even edge along the top and sides with a slight swell at the bottom of the back. Form a roll round the back from the top of one arm to the other by making a *sink* or *blind* stitch all round.

This completes the first stuffing of the chair, and, although it is not seen, it is the vital part upon which the durability and comfort of the job is based.

Settee Having dealt with the webbing, springing, and first stuffing of the easy chairs, we now pass to the settee, since it is generally more economical to plan and cut the cover for the complete suite. The settee is constructed on similar lines to the easies. Apart from minor adjustments, the frame is an enlarged edition of the chair frame. The dimensions of the rails and the width of the arms are the same as for the chairs unless an extra large settee is required. If this is desired extend the width and use two stretcher rails on seat and back equally spaced; also it is advisable to use a heavier front seat rail. The 4ft. 6in., two-seater settee was originally intended for a small room. Most present day bungalows and chalets are planned with large lounges requiring much larger settees, three and four seaters, measuring anything from six to eight feet overall.

Fig. 8 Back and seat webbing.
Note the method of supporting the long webs at the stretcher rails. It is not always possible to check the back webbing completely, but endeavour to obtain a flat, true base for the springs.

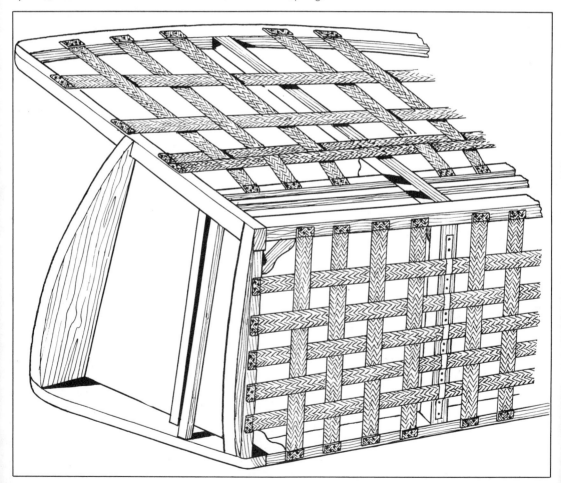

The frame is set out, dowelled and assembled in the same way as the chair frame, but note the stretcher rails in the seat and back. These are essential and must be neatly fitted and dowelled in position. Corner blocks glued and screwed to the rails will help the rigidity of the frame and also provide a suitable place for fitting the castors. Details are given in Fig. 7.

Webbing the seat The first upholstery operation is webbing the seat. Five long webs are required, and these are tacked on first. Start tacking on the left side of the frame as it is turned upside down (viewed from the front). Strain tightly to the right-hand rail and tack down. Follow the same methods as with the webbing of the chair, using $\frac{5}{8}$in. improved tacks, and check the front to back webs under and over. The short webs are tacked on the front rail and strained to the back rail. Work from the centre stretcher rail placing the first web on each side close to this rail. Space the following webs about 43·7mm. (1$\frac{3}{4}$in.) apart. Six good-quality webs each side, on a 1·35m. (4ft. 6in.) settee should be sufficient, with other sizes in proportion. Fig. 8 shows the webbing from the rear.

When the webbing is completed, fold a piece of web in half and tack it across the stretcher rail with two tacks in each space between the long webs. This gives additional support to the webbing at the centre of the seat. The frame is now stood upright on trestles or a similar suitable working base.

Webbing the arms is the next item. Two up and down on each inside arm, are required.

Springing the seat There are eighteen springs in the body of the seat and seven on the front rail, see Fig. 9. The eighteen consist of the two rows of 10in. by 8 gauge, and one row of 9in. by 9 gauge. Set up the springs in three rows from back to front approximately the same as in the chair. The six rows across the seat are arranged with a row each side of the stretcher rail, a row about 1$\frac{1}{2}$in. from each inside arm, and middle rows between the two. The usual three-tie method is used for sewing the springs to the webs. Generally the most convenient starting-point for sewing the springs is from the left side of the front row. It is a matter of personal choice, however, whether the front or back row is dealt with first. With the springs all

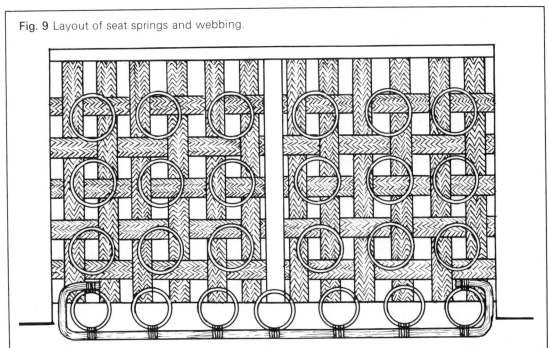

Fig. 9 Layout of seat springs and webbing.

securely sewn to the web the lacing is next, and is an important item. Tack a strip of hessian on the front spring rail. This stops the edge springs from making a noise if one of the rungs hits the rail.

Cut six lengths of laid cord and fix one opposite each row of springs on the back tacking rail. Commence lacing from back to front, bringing the cord to the second rung of the back spring, tying there before passing to the top rung of the same spring. Tie again and continue to the top rung of the middle spring, and tie on both sides. Carry on to the top rung of the front spring and tie on one side, coming down to the second or third rung before tying again. Pull taut to a tack on the front rail. Make sure the springs are correctly positioned before tacking down. Repeat this operation with each row, pulling down each cord to the same degree so that all the tops of the springs are level.

The lengthwise lacings are started from the left side tacking rail. Leave a piece of cord for a return on each tack. Bring the long end of cord to the second or third rung of the first spring then to the top rung. Tie or half-hitch in the usual way and continue over all the springs on the top rungs until the last row. On this row repeat the starting procedure and pull taut to a tack on the tacking rail. The position of the springs should be upright except for the rows nearest the arms. These should lean outwards, that is, to the arms. Ascertain that the positions are correct before bringing the short ends of cord or returns to the top rungs of the end springs.

When the lacing is completed the tops of the springs should form a slight curve from arm to arm. From back to front there should be rather more of a curve with its lowest point at the back. Aim at an even surface, i.e. no one row or spring being higher or lower other than the normal curve.

Front edge springing The front edge springs are the next item, and the methods employed are the same as on the chair front, see Fig. 3. This time seven springs are required instead of four. Place the springs one at each end, one in the middle and the others equally spaced between them. They will be almost between the rows of the main body springs, but it may be necessary to adjust one or two of the laid cord fixing tacks in order to place the edge spring in position. Pull the edge springs over with a web and tie back with laid cord as on the chair. A

piece of cane or 8-gauge wire is bent to the required size, that is about 12.5mm. ($\frac{1}{2}$in.) from the arm uprights at each end. Whip the cane or wire to the front edge of the top coil of each spring and the returns to the back edges of the end springs.

This completed, cover the whole seat with a stout hessian, tucking it down between the front edge springs and the front row of the body springs to form a gutter. Fix this at each end with a tack, pulling the hessian taut. Temporarily fix the remainder of the hessian at the back and sides.

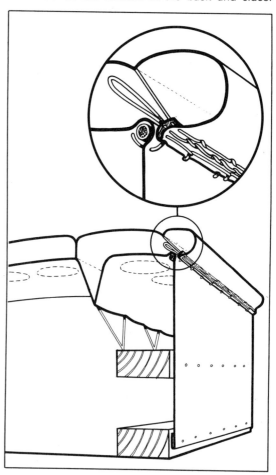

Fig. 10 Sectional view through the seat. The springs are omitted for clarity. This shows how the gutter is formed with the hessian, and the stitches used in making the roll or edge.

Tie the gutter in place with loops of laid cord through the hessian and back to tacks on the spring rail between the springs, see Fig. 10. The front portion of the hessian can then be tacked in place. Tack off on the bottom seat rail, doubling under the edge, and afterwards add a few sparsely spaced tacks through the hessian at the spring rail level. Complete tacking down the hessian round the sides and back, turning over the edges. The tops of the springs and the cane are sewn to the hessian with the usual ties and hitches.

Cut a piece of scrim or hessian to cover the seat and tuck this down at the back. Fix with half a dozen temporary tacks and lay the surplus over the tacking rails out of the way. Fill in the sides and back with fibre and the gutter with hair. Make three or four loops of twine along the top of the front edge hessian and pick an even amount of fibre under them. Fill in the centre of the seat with a thin layer of hair or fibre. Bring the scrim over and fix with skewers under the cane edge. Tuck down at the sides under the arms and temporarily fix. Make three lines of running-through ties on the main part of the seat behind the gutter.

This completed, the stuffing of the edge can be picked over, evened out, and the scrim fixed evenly along the cane with skewers. A fine twine in a half-circular needle is used to sew the scrim to the hessian along the cane. Using a regulator or stout, straight needle regulate the edge stuffing well forward and start stitching the roll or edge. Use a sink stitch first, just along the top of the cane, this pulls the stuffing forward in a firm mass. The edge or roll is completed by a top stitch made as close as possible to the sink stitch on the underside of the scrim and coming through on the top of the seat about 37·5mm. (1½in.) from the edge. Use a regulator frequently to work the stuffing forward, thus forming a firm even edge a little thicker than a man's thumb. Finish the scrim stuffing by tacking down the scrim round the sides and back keeping the stuffing even. Fig. 10 shows a section through the roll.

First stuffing the back The build-up of the settee back is similar to the chair back. All the webbing is tacked on to the back edges of the rails, three webs up and down in each division of the back, six in all; and four webs lengthwise, two close together at the bottom of the back, one approximately 3in. from the top rail and one in the middle of the back. Check the webs as far as possible. Six 6in. by 10-gauge springs are set up and sewn to the bottom webs. Twelve 6in. by 12-gauge springs are sewn to the middle and top positions at the crossing of the webs.

The bottom and middle rows of springs can be held in position by lightly lacing with cord through the centre rungs of each spring. Use one cord only from side to side on each row. Pull the springs of the top row slightly upwards by passing a cord round their middle rungs. Fix to ⅝in. improved tacks on the top rail. Cover the springs with hessian, fixing it in position with temporary tacks before finally tacking down on the front edge of the rails. The tops of the springs are sewn to the hessian with three ties. Cut a piece of scrim or light hessian large enough to cover the back and allowing for the depth of the roll or edge and turnings. Tack a turned-in edge of the scrim on the back tacking rail.

Assuming that the settee is lying on its back on the trestles, pull the scrim out of the way, lay it over the seat, and push a skewer or two through it to keep it there. Proceed with the stuffing of the back. Use fibre round the edges, picked evenly under the usual loops of twine, and fibre or hair, in the centre of the back. Pull the scrim over and fix all round temporarily. Starting at one of the bottom corners complete an oblong with a line through its centre, of long and short running-through ties. These ties can be pulled down fairly tightly, but leave the final tightening until the tacking off and stitching is completed. This is the next operation, to tack off the scrim evenly along the top and two sides of the back. The edge should be a little over 50mm. (2in.) deep before stitching, evenly stuffed but not packed hard with fibre. If it is intended to use hair as the top stuffing a single sink or blind stitch is all that is required. Flock or fibre top stuffing loses its shape more quickly and it would be better to make a small top stitch as well.

Second stuffing The settee and the two easies completed to the first or scrim stuffing stage, the planning and cutting of the covers can be proceeded with. Even in pre-austerity days it was advisable to measure twice before cutting once. It is even more necessary with the present high prices. Double-width material, as it is termed, cuts more economically than single width. It may measure from 1·2m. to 1·3m. (47in. to 52in.) wide.

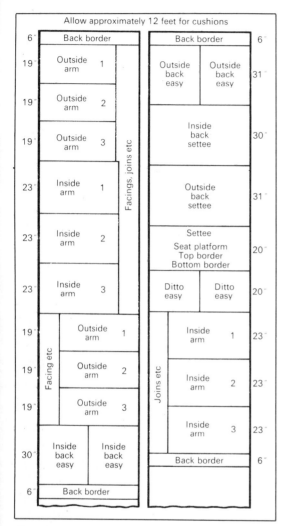

Allow approximately 12 feet for cushions

6″	Back border		Back border		6″
19″	Outside arm	1	Outside back easy	Outside back easy	31″
19″	Outside arm	2			
19″	Outside arm	3	Inside back settee		30″
23″	Inside arm	1	Outside back settee		31″
23″	Inside arm	2			
23″	Inside arm	3	Settee Seat platform Top border Bottom border		20″
			Ditto easy	Ditto easy	20″
19″	Outside arm	1	Inside arm	1	23″
19″	Outside arm	2	Inside arm	2	23″
19″	Outside arm	3	Inside arm	3	23″
30″	Inside back easy	Inside back easy	Back border		6″
6″	Back border				

(vertical labels: Facings, joins etc. · Facing etc. · Joins etc.)

Fig. 11 Suggested layout of the cover.
Note how the arm pieces are cut to pair, and are numbered to avoid mistakes.

Thirty-one inch, generally called single-width, or 36in. materials will need more yardage and more joins. Large patterns and stripes often cut awkwardly and require more material.

All patterns, large or small, should be centred on the seat and back and balanced on the arms. This means trying to cut the two inside and two outside arms so they make a uniform pair. Endeavour to

carry out these methods throughout the suite so that a symmetrical effect is obtained. The seat borders have two rows of piping, thus forming double borders. The seat is fitted and the two borders and piping are machine stitched together.

Piping is made up by cutting strips of cover about 28–31mm. ($1\frac{1}{8}$–$1\frac{1}{4}$in.) wide. The strips are joined together, then folded over with a piping cord or laid cord inserted, and sewn together. Whenever possible cut the piping on the bias as it sets better when sewn. Piping cuts into a lot of material, so save all trimmings and odd pieces. Notes on this are given in Chapter VIII.

Cutting the cover Approximately $16\frac{1}{2}$yds. of 50in. material will be required for the suite if made to the original sizes. The suggested layout of the cover in Fig. 11 is intended as a guide. It does not follow that any particular piece must be cut first. The pattern of the cover and how it will lend itself to the cutting sizes decides the order of cutting. Check the sizes given by measuring with a tape-measure over the actual job. The inside' covers are all flyed. This term means that a piece of hessian or inexpensive material is sewn to the cover along the sides where it is not seen when pushed through between the arms and seat, or back and seat. The flys are really extensions of the main cover and are used for tacking down in the unseen positions. An example of how the cover can be flyed is given in Fig. 12.

Covering the seat A lining is generally used on the seats over the part covered by the cushions. Draw a line across the seats at six inches inwards from the front edge of the roll. A piece of cover is cut at 7 inches wide to cover this portion of the seat termed the front platform. The back section is to be covered with a colour matching piece of lining. This is joined to the cover platform piece, also a piece of wide tape or webbing is stitched along this join. Lay the completed platform on the seat and pin in position with several skewers. Cut the corners to shape not omitting the sewing allowance. Make a chalk or pencil line along the front hessian where the border piping join will be sewn. Join up the two border pieces with the piping inserted. Remove the platform cover from the seat and join up with the borders, also with a piping inserted. Replace the cover on the seat tucking the tape under the arms and fixing tautly

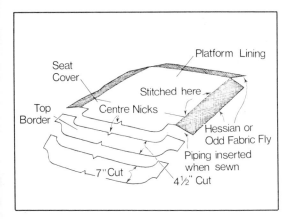

Fig. 12 How seat cover is flyed, see also side joints.
The notches show the centre when cover is being worked into position.

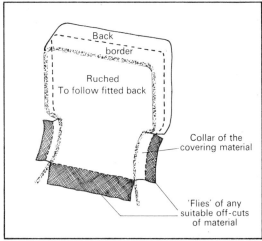

Fig. 13 Back cover ready to place in position.

on the seat rails each side. Stitch through this tape with a series of long stitches using either a half-circular needle or a 10in. mattress needle and twine. Make two or three loops of twine along the top border section, the front seat section and the back portion. Pick a very light amount of hair on to the back section, cover with lintafelt and pull the lining over, pushing it under the arms and back rails, fixing on the seat rails.

Continue with a slightly heavier amount of hair on the front part and on the top border section. Pull the cover over, not forgetting the lintafelt, and fix with skewers at the line on the hessian. Sew to the hessian along the line with a half-circular needle and twine. When completed, finish off the bottom border with a good thickness of lintafelt, tacking off on the underside of the seat rail.

Arms It is proposed to use a fibre or hessian pad for the arms. Tack this along the bottom tacking rail pulling it up and over to the outer edge of the top arm rail. Tack down on the top rail near the edge leaving a good three inches overhanging. Continue in the same way down the arm upright. Finish tacking off straight on the back upright. Roll over the surplus 3in. along the top edge and on the upright to form a finger size roll firmly tacked off on the top of the rails, but overhanging on the outer edges. Three loops of twine across the centre of the pad and three across the top rail are made to pick

the hair under and hold it in place. Fibre can be used or rubberized hair laid on but a thin layer of hair below the top rail and a good thickness on the top rail covered with linterfelt will make a nice arm.

When starting to cover lay the linterfelt over the fibre roll to give a bold and soft effect, as it is intended to finish the arms with covered wood facings. Tuck the fly of the inside arm cover under the arm tacking rail, fixing it in position with 3 or 4 temporary tacks. Pull up and over to the underside of the top arm rail again temporarily tacking. Smooth out and fix on the front facing and on the back upright. Repeat this procedure cleaning out the cover and pulling taut before starting to tack down on the underside of the top arm rail. Continue down the facing and the back upright. The bottom fly can be tacked on the seat rail over the seat cover.

Back The inside backs are also fitted on the job. They are to be bordered around the top sections and fitted with collars around the arms. Cut off a cover length and lay it over the scrim stuffing fixing it all round with skewers. Mark along the top and two sides also around each arm. Fit the top and side borders approx. in place and make a few nicks opposite each other on both borders and centre piece. Cut around the arms to make a good fit and insert collar pieces to meet the border. The back and borders can be finished either with a piping or a ruche. Ruching looks more luxurious and can be machined to the back and borders the same as piping. The bottom of the backs can be *flyed* on the bottom edges to save cover. Before sewing the first inside back use it as a pattern to cut the second one. The settee will have to be cut separately whether a two or three seater, using the same methods of fitting. Top stuff the back with hair covered with linterfelt and place a layer of linterfelt round the top and two sides where bordered. With the inside arms and seat covered and tacked down, continue with the inside back using the same methods to fix in position, smooth out and tack off.

Outside arms and backs The outside arms are fixed along the undersides of the top arm rails over the tacked off edge of the inside arms. After fixing correctly in place the cover is backed tacked to give a clean finish. Cut a 18·75mm. ($\frac{3}{4}$in.) strip of buckram or cardboard and place this along the underside of the outside arm where it is to be tacked off on the top rail. The tacks are driven through the cardboard clear of the edge so a clean straight line is obtained when the outside arm is pulled down and tacked off on the underside of the seat rail. Temporary fix the front edge on the front facing. Tack off the back edge on the outside back upright. The outside backs are finished in a similar manner at the top.

Should a light or loosely woven cover be used it is often advisable to line the outside arms and backs. Use a light hessian and tack or staple on the outside rails before pulling the outside covers over to tack down. It is proposed to finish the front of the arm with a covered wood facing. A piece of 6·25mm. ($\frac{1}{4}$in.) ply cut to shape to cover the tacking off on the front upright is required. The other outer edges are rounded off and three small holes for screws are drilled to fix it in place. A layer of linterfelt is laid on the ply and the cover is fixed over it tacking off on the back. Make up some piping and tack it round the facing on the back edge. Leave both the outer edge of the cover and the piping floating so it can be lifted up and the screws inserted and driven home. The outer edge of the facing cover is tacked off on the main arm upright, also the piping and the outside arm cover is brought up to the piping, turned in and slip-stitched for a clean finish.

Thicker polished wood facings can be dowelled in

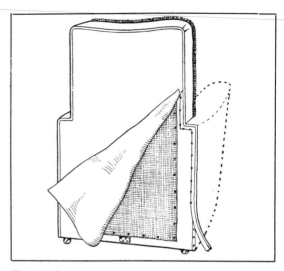

Fig. 14 Outside back, showing hessian lining, piping etc.

place or thin covered ply ones can be panel pinned through a soft cover if carefully done. With the covering of the chair completed it can now be turned up and a 'bottom' of light hessian or a black lining neatly turned in and tacked or stapled all round. A set of castors of a suitable type can also be fitted before turning the chair upright again.

Cushion This leaves the cushion as the last operation. Cushions can be of latex foam, *Polyfoam*, foam covered with *Dacron* or similar wadding, or feathers and down mixtures. First, a paper templet must be taken of the size and shape of the seat. Mark this all round and cut to shape. Allow for the thickness of the ruche or piping. Lay the templet on the cover and cut the cover to it, not omitting a sewing allowance all round. Cut the box borders to size according to the unit being used, plus sewing allowance. Foam latex units should be covered in a light calico. Feathers of all grades require a downproof cambric case preferably made up with two divisions crossways to form three compartments, thereby keeping the feathers where they are most needed. On this type of chair feathers and down mixtures can give a most comfortable seat, possibly only equalled by the *Dacron* over foam unit which returns to shape quicker than feathers after use.

Make up the cushion cover inserting either ruche or piping all round the top and bottom pieces and

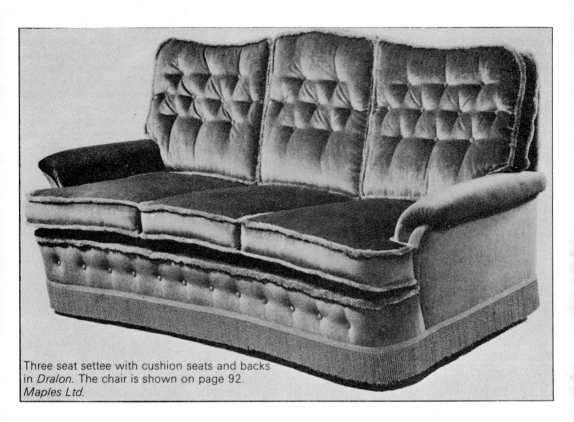

Three seat settee with cushion seats and backs in *Dralon*. The chair is shown on page 92. *Maples Ltd.*

join up with the borders. The back border can be cut as two narrow pieces and a zip fastener inserted between them to form the closure. Insert the required cushion unit into the case, thereby completing the chair. Continue with the settee using the same methods only on a larger scale. According to its length two, three or four cushions may be needed. This same set of frames can be fully upholstered with polyether foam on patent sprung seat units and serpentine back springing. The back seat tacking rails can be increased in size to 50mm. by 37·5mm. (2in. by 1½in.) and cut well into the back uprights to prevent turning through the tension of the spring units when fitted. A single spring unit preferably of the spring base type as shown on page 20 makes a good seat base. Fix with one inch clout nails to the front spring rail and the back seat rail. Cover with either a hessian pad or plain hessian and 1½in. foam. Place the seat cover in position as described in the hand-sprung details. The arms are hessianed the same and an inch

piece of foam can be stapled or tacked on to the top arm rail cutting it to the shape of the rail. Lay a 12·50mm. (½in.) piece of foam from the bottom tacking rail right over this foam and the arm rail to the under edge. Cover as for the bespoke suite. The backs can be sprung with serpentine springing approx. four inches apart fixed, on the bottom back tacking rail and pulled up to the top back rail. It is advisable to lace the springs with a laid cord from side to side. Two cords at a third and two thirds down from the top rail, knotting each spring as it crosses. Lay a piece of hessian over the springs tacking down all round. A 75mm. (3in.) thick block of foam of light density is required to give a soft, bold looking back on this frame. A thinner piece of foam can be used if the top back rail is turned round so its widest thickness is uppermost. The top sections of the back uprights being boxed up with fillets to even them up with the top rail. The foam can be fixed to the hessian with an adhesive round the top and sides for about two inches inwards or an adhesive tape can be used round the top and sides and tacked or stapled to the edges of these rails. The covering of the back is carried out the same as on the hair stuffed backs. It is suggested that these backs with thick foam will keep their shapes better if a few buttons are inserted, a single row across the centre just above the line from arm to arm, or a half diamond in a similar position. A full diamond would start an inch or so lower. The cushions would be the same as previously described.

Cushion backs A further suggestion for upholstering this suite would be to make loose foam cushions on the backs. The back could be webbed with rubber webbing, loosely hessianed or the hessian omitted. A piece of one inch foam stapled or tacked over the webbing and covered in the ordinary way. Cut a piece of light density 100mm. (4in.) foam to fit over the arms and to stand about two inches above the top of the back. Cut and make up a cover to fit the foam. Button it with four buttons spaced as a large square.

Chapter eighteen

Contemporary Three-Piece Suite

Despite increasing mass production methods in upholstered furniture there is still a vast range of designs from which to choose one's own particular style of comfort. Modern, contemporary, exotic, blown up, tied up, they all have a spasm.

There is one type which seems to hold its own against all comers. The wing easy chair has been changing its style and shape since the days of Queen Anne, but it is still with us in many forms. The suite in Fig. 1 is not of the latest design but is simple and easy to alter if so desired. It was originally designed for the older stuffings but foam can be easily substituted.

Frames Close-grained, sound timber is required for the frames. North American birch used to be the most favoured wood, but is difficult to obtain now. A good beech is quite suitable, and other close-grained timbers are equally useful. Some of the newer timbers being introduced do not take tacks too well, several tacks in a line causing splits. Dowels 9·4mm. ($\frac{3}{8}$in.) diam. are used on all joints except those on the front ends of the seat-springing rails; mortise and tenon joints are recommended

Fig. 1 Simple modern suite with loose cushions.

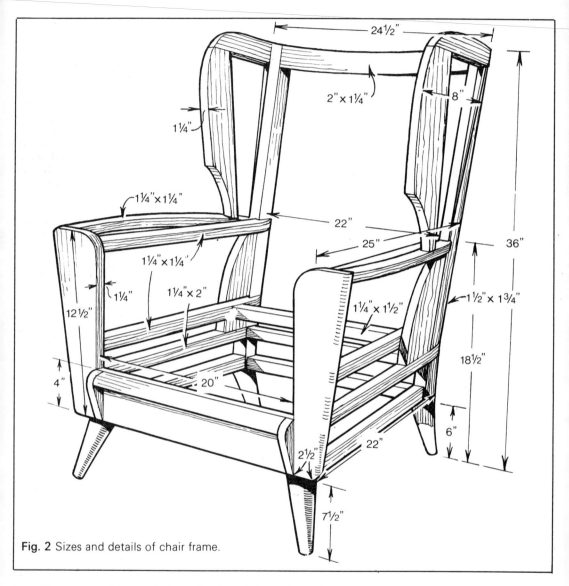

Fig. 2 Sizes and details of chair frame.

here. The arm uprights or facings, back uprights, and all side rails are the same on both chairs and settee, the front and back rails making the difference in width between chairs and settee.

Cut the arm upheads and the front rail, bore for four $\frac{3}{8}$in. dowels in each end of the front seat rail. Also bore the backs of the upheads for the arm and side rails, and cut the mortises for the seat-spring-

ing rails. The settee side rails can be dowelled as the springing is from back to front. Use the same method with the back upheads, marking out and boring the dowel holes for both the back-cross rails and side rails. After this has been completed assemble the back framing.

When the glue on both the front and back sections has set, assemble the frame complete with the side

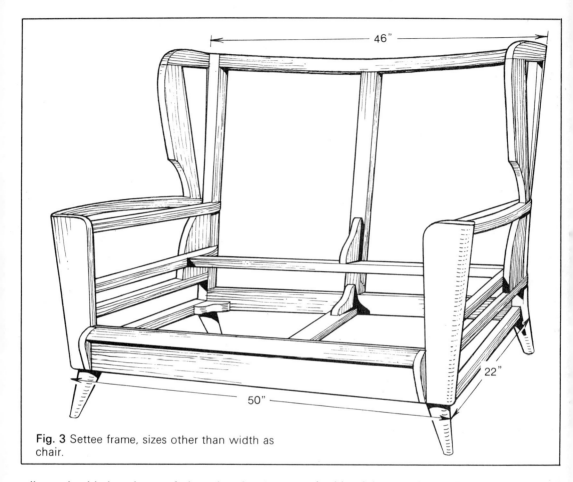

Fig. 3 Settee frame, sizes other than width as chair.

rails, and add the pieces of the wing framing. Finally fit the front legs. These are rounded and tapered and also set at the slight angle as shown. Fix in position with 6·25mm. (¼in.) bolts. Alternatively, ready-turned legs with various fixing devices can be bought for the front legs.

Note that the outer edges of all members which could chafe the upholstery fabric are rounded off.

Springing Nine ½in. diameter tension springs are used in each easy-chair seat (eighteen in the settee seat) and 9·4mm. (⅜in.) diameter for the backs. Before starting the upholstery mark out and cut to shape six pieces of plywood to fit the top of the arms, so that the straight edge rests on the top of the inside straight rail and the curved edge fits the

underside of the outside rail: the ply is then glued and nailed on.

Arms Now for the actual upholstery. Tack two webs on each arm, spacing the first about 250mm. (10in.) from the front and the other near the back upright, one end being tacked on at the lower tacking rail and stretched to the top rail. Use ½in. improved tacks for the webs and also for the hessian which is tacked on next over the webs. Strain both webs and hessian tightly when tacking off except at the back uprights, where it is left loose but long enough to tack down on the uprights later. The plywood-covered space on the top of the arms is filled in with some loose fibre or hair stuffing, and covered with the extending piece of hessian.

Fix the back springs in position using either of the

methods shown to hold them in place. Use two $\frac{1}{2}$in. diameter springs on the lower part of the backs, four on the settee back. Fill in the top portions with the $\frac{3}{8}$in. springs spaced approximately 75mm. (3in.) apart, keeping the top one as near the top as possible. Cover this springing with a fibre or hair pad, that is, hair or fibre woven on to hessian. Another method would be to use hessian over the springs and rubberized hair laid on the hessian. In either case hold it in place with a few tacks at the top and bottom rails.

Wings The wings are webbed and hessianed in the same way as the arms, a web being stretched from the top arm rail to the top of the wing close to the back upright. Tack the hessian on the wing framing and pull the back edge through the space between the web and upright. Fix on to the uprights with three or four tacks, and make several ties with twine along the web to hold the hessian to it. This completed, the fixing tacks can be released so the space is open again. The loose edge of hessian will be tacked off later when the wing is covered. Unless the side seat rails have been grooved for rings as illustrated, use plates for fixing the seat springs. These are bored at 50mm. (2in.) spacing for the springs and are screwed into a rebate on the top of the rails Pirelli or similar rubber webbing can be used instead of springs and a lining would not be needed over the web. The chairs have now reached the stage when the cover can be cut and fitted, and the settee should be dealt with in a similar way.

Cutting the Cover Present trends in covering fabrics tends to be of the plain type, or at least not set patterned, but there is no reason why a patterned material should not be used on the insides and a plain one on the outsides.

Before cutting a patterned material, plan the cover so that there is a centre pattern on the seat cushion and inside backs. Measure each section of the suite with a tape measure allowing 12·5mm. ($\frac{1}{2}$in.) for all sewing edges and about an inch for turning when tacking down. After cutting the inside and outside arms fix one of each on an arm with fixing tacks.

Cut each to shape to fit the arm, notching at several points, remove from the arm and cut the remaining five arms from these templates, not forgetting the notches or to pair the three sets of arms. Join up

the inside and outside arms with a piping between them—the piping can be made up first using a 37·5mm. (1$\frac{1}{2}$in.) strip of material with a piece of cord inserted. The centre portion of each seat can be covered with a lining starting about 150mm. (6in.) inwards from the front edge. Allow the front cover to come from the first spring over the front rail down to the bottom rail, tacking off on the underside, and cut this front piece wide enough to tack off on the side rails.

Join to the lining leaving 150mm. (6in.) of lining under the cover: this will come under No. 1 spring. Fix in place temporarily and cut the sides of the front cover to fit the front. Also cut two small borders or side facings to fit the sides of the front cover. Remove from the frame and join up with a piping inserted. The inside backs, inside and outside wings are straightforward cuts, no fitting for piping being required.

Make certain there is sufficient cover for the cushions and borders but do not cut the cushions until the suite is covered as a template is needed to obtain a well-fitting cushion.

Covering Start the covering proper with the seats. The platform lining attached to the front edge covering is laid on the seat; pass the loose extending piece of lining under No. 1 tension spring and tack it down on the front edge rail. Tack a piece of hessian over the lining and pass it back under the first spring and over, back to the front edge again, continuing down to the lower front rail. Place several layers of linter's felt on the hessian and pull the front cover over it, fixing it with temporary tacks. Stretch the lining over the springs to the back tacking rail and the side rails. Tack this down all round but do not pull it taut sideways, and leave sufficient play to allow for the expansion of the springs in use; clean the front portion of rucks and finally tack off.

Although the settee seat springs are fixed from back to front the seat covering can be carried out in a similar manner, but with this difference—there is no spring from side to side to pull the lining and hessian under. Therefore stretch a folded web from side rail to side rail at the same distance as the spring is on the easy frame and use it as a spring for holding the cover in place.

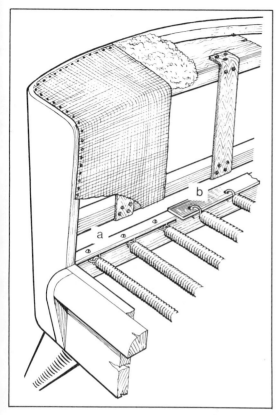

Fig. 4 Upholstery of arm.
Alternative methods of fixing seat springs are shown.

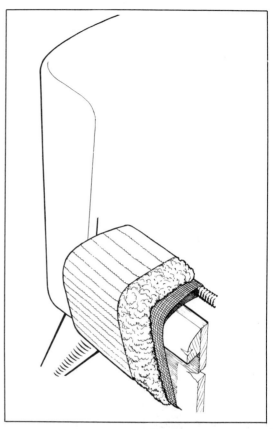

Fig. 5 Front of seat.
Note hessian taken round first spring and back.

Arm covering Cover the arms next, using a layer of 1 in. rubberized hair or a sheet of foamed latex 1 in. thick. Whichever is being used, cut to shape and fix in place, using a spot of impact adhesive here and there to hold it in position. The hair can be held with tacks along the edges and should be graduated off to the lower tacking rails. A layer of linter's felt is required over hair, but it is not necessary over latex sheeting. Lay the fitted cover over gently, and gradually draw it over into position, holding it in place with a few fixing tacks. Clean out and tack off on the lower tacking rails but leave free on the outsides. Complete both arms to this stage before starting on the back.

Whether rubberized hair, hair pads, or fibre pads are used, two good layers of linter's felt will be needed to obtain really good backs. Before placing the linter's felt on the back, tuck the lower end of the inside back cover through the tacking rails and fix on the back tacking rail with about three temporary tacks. Lay the remainder of the cover back on the seat. Place the linter's felt in position, and draw the back over to the top rail fixing there and down the sides on the uprights: pull taut and clean all round, but not so tightly as to spoil the shape, and tack off. Tie in three buttons equally spaced across the back of each easy in a line about level with the top of the arm (five are used across the settee back). Use a mattress needle and twine, pulling down tight with a slip-knot.

The wings can be all linter's felt, a good thick double layer. Fix the cover on the back upright and

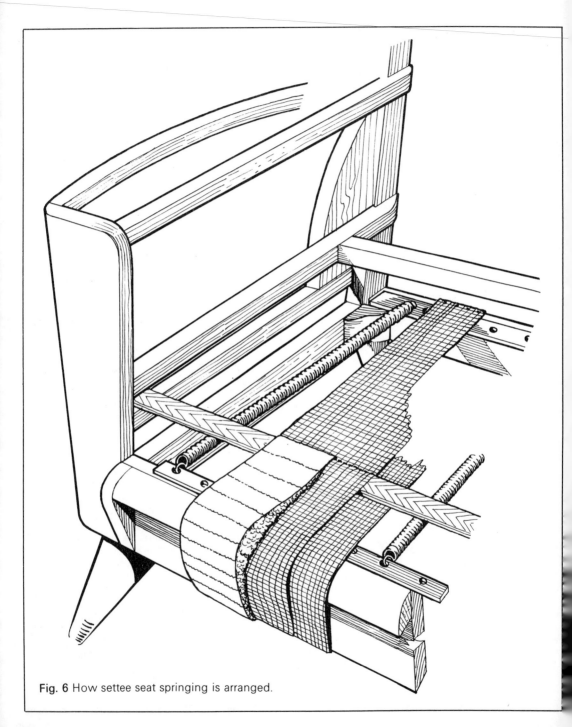

Fig. 6 How settee seat springing is arranged.

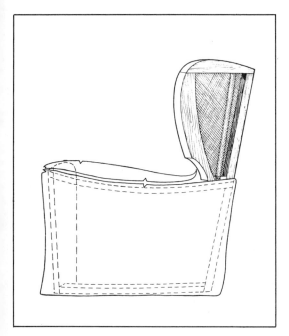

Fig. 7 Cutting and fitting inside and outside arms.

pull over to the front, then clean out upwards and downwards, using temporary tacks until all rucks are cleaned out. Tack down but do not pull down too hard as it spoils the comfort of a soft wing.

Outside Having completed the covering of the front of the chair or settee, the outsides and finishing off can be proceeded with. Make up some lengths of piping and tack it round the front edges of the wings and the top of the back. Use fine tacks, either ⅜in. or ½in., for tacking off the covers. Fix the outside wings along the front edges close to the piping, tack off at the lower edge on the arm rail and on the back uprights, the piping on the top of the outside arm being pulled across the wing and tacked on the rear side of the back upright. Similarly, the outside arm is also tacked off all round, pulling the fabric taut and clean.

Complete the tacking off of the outside wings and arms before proceeding with the outside backs, which are back-tacked along the top of the top back rail close to the piping and pulled to the lower rail, tacking off on the underside. The side edges are turned in and can be gimp-pinned

down or preferably slip-stitched. Use a small half circular needle and strong carpet thread making tight stitches not too close together. Finish the outside wings by slip-stitching and the lower part of the arms where they finish below the seat level. A calico or light hessian bottom completes the upholstery.

The legs could be finished with black polish, preferably a dull or satin black. Flat castors of the 'quad' type could be fitted, or the brass ferrules with an adjustable toe which give and elegant finishing touch.

Cushions Take a template of the seats with stiff paper, and lay it on the cover allotted for the cushions: cut round the template, leaving 9·4mm. or 12·5mm. (⅜in. or ½in.) sewing allowance all round. Foamed latex cushions are suggested as being the most suitable and you should cut the borders fairly tightly so that a smart cushion is obtained. If there is enough cover to cut the piping on the cross or bias it will be worth while doing so as it gives a much better finish to the cushions.

Fabric Cutting List

Use 50in. wide material. Inside and outside measurements are given separately so that a two-colour scheme can be used. All sizes are approximate, and it is advisable to check against the actual job.

Inside arms, settee and easies	19in. × half width
Inside back settee	33in. × full width
Inside back easy	33in. × half width
Seat and border, settee	14in. × full width
Seat and border, easy	14in. × half width
Inside wings	17½in. × 12in.
Cushions, tops and bottoms	21in. × 21in.
Cushion borders	4½in. × full width
Outside arms and wings	16in. × 32in. 16in. × 10in.
Outside backs	32in. × full width 32in. × half width

Piping from surplus from wings and widths plus ½ yard, making 9 yards for insides, and 4½ yards for outsides.

A good example of a nicely buttoned Chesterfield
by *R. Tyzack Ltd.*

Chapter nineteen

A Well-Cushioned Suite

The suite in Fig. 1 is an up-to-date design, streamlined, devoid of gimmicks, and nicely proportioned. Not only is the design modern but it is intended to be built up with the pick of modern materials. All show-wood parts of the frames are of teak, a fashionable timber at present. It is a strong, durable timber much used in boatbuilding, resistant to worm, and does not need polishing. An occasional drop of oil rubbed in will help to retain its natural look for a long, long time.

The covered woodwork can be plywood or particle board with supporting rails of beech or birch. Sizes can be varied if desired but the 1·84m. (6ft. 1½in.) settee gives comfortable seating for three persons. Cut out the main frame members to size and clean up before assembling. Dowel joints are usual in frame making; three dowels on the main rails and two on the smaller rails. Use a good glue and cramp up tightly when assembling. Clean off surplus glue, particularly on the show-wood joints. Note that the back seat rail is set in from the rear and is tenoned into the side rails,

Fig. 1

When working with hand cramps it is usually advisable to assemble the arms first. Join up with the seat front and back rails, and finally add the back supporting rail. Fig. 2 gives the main sizes.

Build up of the arms The upholstery on the arms is built up separately on 18·75mm. or 25mm. (¾in. or 1in.) particle board. There are two pieces joined at right angles to form an inverted L shape, glued and screwed, the bottom piece to meet the front rail and to fix on the side rail when covered. The top piece, 125mm. (5in.) wide, will rest on the top arm rail. Lay a 12·5mm. (½in.) piece of foam over the whole of the arm, holding it in place with a few dabs of adhesive. On the top of the arm add a 25mm. (1in.) thick piece of poly-foam.

Complete the building up of the arms before cutting the cover for them. The inside arm is covered straight over both foam and base boards and tacked off on the underside of the base boards. The top arm portion covers the whole underside of the top piece as this will be seen, excepting where it rests on the arm rail. Likewise, the bottom piece is covered up to the top arm on the underside.

Backs Make up the backs from 12·5mm. (½in.) ply, 525mm. by 525mm. (21in. by 21in.) for the centre piece, 525mm. by 625mm. (21in. by 25in.) side settee pieces, and 525mm. by 650mm. (21in. by 26in.) each easy chair, these being shaped round the arms. Glue and screw a fillet approximately 25mm. by 25mm. (1in. by 1in.) to the inside bottom of each piece of ply. These back boards are screwed to the back support rail and the bottom seat rail after the cushions have been fitted and covered. Building up the basic framework of the settee must be completed before the back and arm sections can be fitted.

Two substantial stretcher rails are needed across the settee seat from front to back. These should be set below the level of the front and back rails and well curved so that they allow the rubber webbing to give. They are tenoned into the rails and must be added when the whole frame is assembled. a 25mm. by 37·5mm. (1in. by 1½in.) tacking rail should be temporarily screwed to the inside of the front rail.

Space the rubber webbing, which forms the base of the seat, onto this rail. Eighteen webs 50mm.

(2in.) wide spaced six in each division of the settee are use, and six to each chair seat. Rubber webbing can be obtained cut to size with metal plates at each end. These ends are inserted into grooves cut into the seat rails for this purpose, but it will probably be difficult to obtain these webs in small quantities. Therefore, the method suggested is to tack the web on to the front tacking rail with large headed tacks or small clouts. Cut the lengths of web required. Approximately 10% stretch is needed but allow sufficient length to obtain a grip on the end of each web with web nippers so that it can be pulled into position and tacked down. Remove the tacking rail from the front seat rail and tack one end of each web on the back of the rail equally spaced. Replace the rail screwing on tightly with the webs hanging over the top of the rail. Stretch each web to the back rail, tacking off well to the rear of the rail and leaving at least ¼in. beyond the tacks.

A piece of lining to cover the webs can be cut 50mm. (2in.) larger than the seats and hemmed all round. Stitch a short length of narrow width elastic at each back corner and three in between on the settee. These elastics are tacked to the back seat rail after the front hem has been back-tacked along the tacking rail. Don't pull the lining or elastics too tightly as they must give when the webs are depressed by being sat upon.

The back boards can be fitted and temporarily screwed in position. Screw the bottom fillets to the back seat rail and bore through the back supporting rail, two screws to each piece of ply.

The upholstery filling With the frames completed we come to the upholstery which is all foam. The two main types of foam are latex rubber and polyether. Latex is more resilient, regaining its shape more quickly than the polyether; also it is more expensive. Polyether is a manufactured foam made in several densities by many firms, some of the top grades getting very close to latex rubber. It is suggested that this suite is upholstered with latex foam seat cushions, polyether back cushions and arms.

The seat cushions are all 550mm. deep by 525mm. (22in. deep by 21in.) wide by 87·5mm. (3½in.) border domed to approximately 112·5mm. (4½in.) centres. Back cushions of polyether cut to fit around the arms and all extending above the back

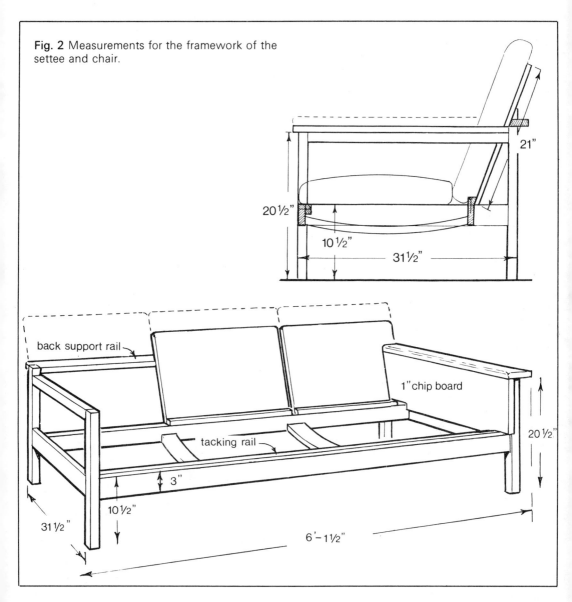

Fig. 2 Measurements for the framework of the settee and chair.

21"

20½"

10½"

31½"

back support rail

1"chip board

tacking rail

3"

20½"

31½"

10½"

6'-1½"

plys by approximately 87·5mm. (3½in.). A 100mm. (4in.) thickness of foam should finish about 87·5mm. (3½in.) in depth when buttoned and tacked off. Cover the arms with foam as previously described and measure over the arms for covering.

Cover Having reached the stage when the measurements can be taken and the cover cut to size, it has to be decided the style of finish required. One method is to finish the cushions with piped borders all round; also the arm facings. Another way is to plain seam all round. This is becoming more popular with the present vogue for plain covers. Also a plain seam sets better on foams. With the older forms of stuffings seams bedded into the stuffing easily, but a four layered piped seam on foam is apt to stand proud, or work round to a wrong position.

Cut the inside and outside arms as described, and fit and cut the facing. Lay the cover over one of the arms and lightly temporarily tack in place. Offer up the facing and cut to shape making about two notches on both facing and arm cover before removing. Remove from the frame and cut all six to pattern then sew to fit the notches. Cut the shaped back cushions to fit in a similar way. The straight centre settee back cushion and the seat cushions can all be cut to measurements. Leave 12·5mm. (½in.) sewing allowance on all cuts that require seaming. An opening must be left on the backs of the seat cushions through which to insert the cushion unit. If this is fitted with a zip fastener it will make the removal of covers for cleaning or changing easier than slip-stitching on every occasion.

The back cushions also have boxed borders, but carry on the front panel measurement to include the bottom border as there is no need to seam this separately. The side and top borders are joined up to the front panels, and the back panels are joined along the top borders and about 100mm. (4in.) down the side borders. The rest of the way the side borders are tacked on the back of the ply and the outside back panel is brought over and slip-stitched down the sides and tacked off on the underside of the ply at the bottom. Before this is done the ply must be marked out for the buttons and a small hole bored at each marking. The cover is also marked with chalk to correspond, approximately 187·4mm. (7½in.) from the top border seam to the first button, the same to the next row, and about 162·5mm. (6½in.) apart widthways.

Screw the fillets on the bottom of the ply to the back seat rail in their correct places. Lay the bottom of the front panels on the fillets and back tack along the bottom. The cushion unit can now be placed in position and the cushion cover brought up over the cushion. (If the cushion tends to slide use a little adhesive to hold it). Make sure the cushion is in place and the cover fits at the corners before buttoning through the ply to the front cover.

Picking up the button there and returning through the same hole, tying a slip-knot, and fastening it round a tack. Complete all the buttons and pull down to the same level before driving the tacks home. Further notes on buttoning are given in Chapter 23. Before completing the backs the arms must be all covered and fixed in place. The tacking off of both inside and outside arms is completed on the undersides of the chipboard so it is covered by the rails of the main frame. The arms are held in position by three screws through the top arm rail of the main frame, screwed up from underneath. Also three screws through bottom of the inside arm into the side seat rail. Set the arms in position approximately 12·5mm. (½in.) projecting over the show-wood arm at the front.

These all completed the outside backs can be finished as previously mentioned. All that remains is to insert the cushion units in the cases. These can be buttoned if desired but latex foam does not really need buttoning. Foam latex cushion units should always be covered in a light calico. This will help to avoid cover slippage. It will also prevent trouble caused by the adhesives used with foam for joining up etc.

A modern chair design by Kuokhoi Chan, made in France.

Chapter twenty

Box Ottoman

The idea of the box ottoman is old, but there are many modern variations of the notion of making a box with an upholstered lid. The box forms a dust-proof storage for clothes and linen, whilst the top or lid makes a comfortable seat. It can also be used as an emergency bed for a child. A useful all-round size is 1·275m. (4ft. 3in.) long over-all by 550mm. (1ft. 10.) wide, with an inside depth of almost 225mm. (9in.).

Making the box Make up the box to the required size, dovetailing the ends to the sides or, as usually happens in commercial jobs, gluing and nailing them. The head-rest is cut to shape and dowelled to the box. Stiffen each corner with a triangular-sectioned fillet glued and screwed in position. For the framing use 22mm. ($\frac{7}{8}$in.) planed softwood; the bottom can be a piece of 9·4mm. ($\frac{3}{8}$in.) ply. The lid construction depends upon the method of upholstery. If the traditional sprung type is to be followed it can be made with a frame of 87·5mm. by 22mm. ($3\frac{1}{2}$in. by $\frac{7}{8}$in.) stuff with 75mm. by 22mm. (3in. by $\frac{7}{8}$in.) spring rails as in Fig. 2. The modern method, however, is to use

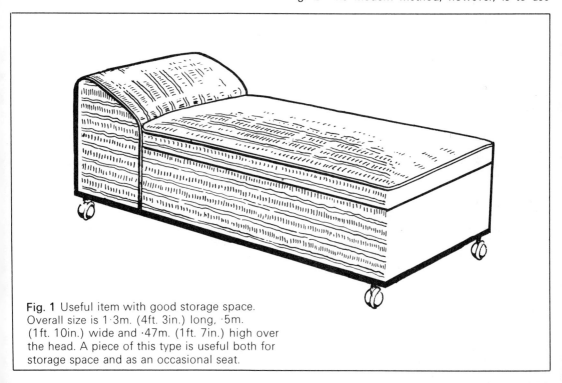

Fig. 1 Useful item with good storage space. Overall size is 1·3m. (4ft. 3in.) long, ·5m. (1ft. 10in.) wide and ·47m. (1ft. 7in.) high over the head. A piece of this type is useful both for storage space and as an occasional seat.

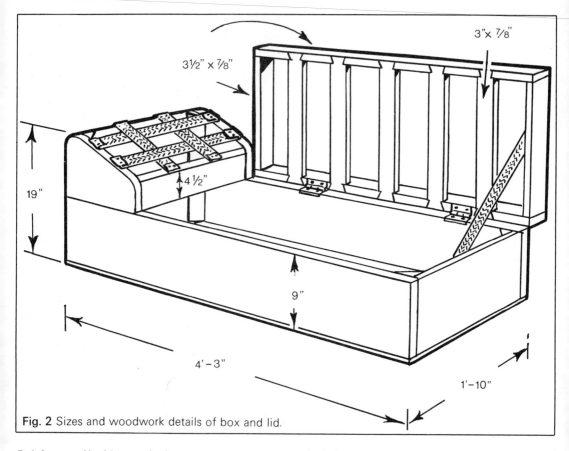

Fig. 2 Sizes and woodwork details of box and lid.

Polyfoam and in this case the framework needs only two intermediate rails with a sheet of plywood nailed on top. This is shown in Fig. 3. For the former system three 5in. by 11 gauge springs are stapled to each rail, with a piece of hessian or soft material tacked on the rails first to form an anti-knock. It is advisable to lace the springs in position with a laid cord. Cover them with a fairly stout hessian, tacking it on temporarily before finally tacking down with ½in. improved tacks. Keep the tacks close to the outside edge of the framing and leave about 62·5mm. (2½in.) of hessian overhanging. Sew the springs to the hessian with the usual three ties.

Top stuffing Lay a small quantity of fibre on the overhanging piece of hessian and roll it over to form an even roll or edge about the size of the thumb. This is continued all round the edge and is

tacked down with ⅝in. tacks. A series of loops of twine are made all round the lid just inside this roll. A top stuffing of hair, flock, or fibre is picked under these loops, also over the central portion of the seat. Cover the whole with a light hessian or calico. This is temporarily fixed in position and finally tacked off on the outside of the framing.

The head is the next item. Tack on and strain two webs each way, using ⅝in. improved tacks. A piece of hessian is tacked over the webs, being strained on as tightly as possible. Make the usual loops of twine round the edge and pick a thin layer of stuffing under them. Cover with hessian or calico similarly to the seat.

Lining the box Lining, or covering the inside of the box must now be dealt with. A strong cotton material is most suitable if obtainable. Remove the

106

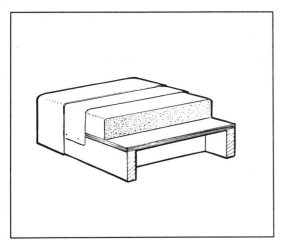

Fig. 3

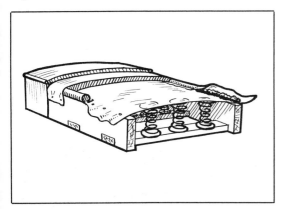

Fig. 4 Sectional view through lid.
This shows springs, hessian, thumb rolls, top stuffing, calico, linter's felt, and cover with piped edge.

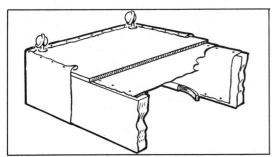

Fig. 5 Details of lining, box shown upside down.

bottom boards before starting the lining, as it is tacked on the bottom edge of the box framing. Start by cutting four strips to cover the corner fillets. Tack these on the bottom and pull as tight as possible to the top edges.

Only three or four tacks will be required on the sides of these corner pieces, provided they are strained on tightly. Continue with the sides and ends in a similar manner, tacking on the bottom edge and straining to the top. At the point where the fillet linings are met do not tack, but fold under and crease well. Then strain as tightly as possible top and bottom and the lining will remain in place without tacking. The bottom piece of lining is laid over the open space of the bottom and tacked on all round the box framing. Details are given in Fig. 5.

The outside cover The lining completed, the outer cover is the next operation, but first replace and fix the bottom. The outer cover is started on the inside of the box about 12·5mm. ($\frac{1}{2}$in.) down. Cut some 12·5mm. ($\frac{1}{2}$in.) strips of cardboard and back-tack through these strips. Draw the cover over the top edge and tack off on the bottom. Repeat this procedure with both sides and one end.

The head is covered separately as it is cut to shape and piped. Cut the top panel to size and the two side panels or facings, allowing $\frac{1}{2}$in. all round for sewing. Piping is sewn along the top and two sides of both facings and the top panel is joined to them.

Lay a piece of wadding or linter's felt over the head and pull the cover over. Tack it off at the back and front, also through the piping seams at the sides. This is done by throwing the two facings back over the head so that it is possible to tack through the seams. The facings are turned back and fixed in place. Tack off on the bottom and along the outside edges. The other edges must be slip-stitched to the main side cover. Finish the outside end by back-tacking along the top edge and slip-stitching the sides to the piping on the facings. Turn the ottoman over and cover the bottom with hessian neatly turned in and tacked. Fix four ball castors beneath.

Cover The cover can be made up with a piping round the top edge or pulled over in one piece and the corners folded in. Whichever way is decided upon a layer of wadding is the first requirement.

Pull the cover over and fix in place all round, finally tacking off on the underside of the lid. This completed, the inside of the lid is lined with the same lining as the box interior. Tack a piece of light hessian over the spring rails and place a thin layer of wadding or linter's felt on the hessian. The lining can then be tacked on using $\frac{1}{2}$in. gimp pins all round, or it may be back-tacked along the front edge and gimp-pinned on the remaining edges.

If latex or polyfoam is to be used, place it on the ply and fix it in place with an adhesive tape or a contact adhesive. Cover all over with a cheap calico before the final cover is pulled over. The final cover is drawn taughtly all round and tacked off on the underside.

A small tab of the covering material can be made, or a fancy handle fitted for lifting the lid if desired. The final operations are fitting the hinges and a staying tape or light chain to prevent the lid over-balancing when in the open position.

A three-seater settee with arms from the 'Duo' unit range. Made in separate units with deep foam cushions. *G-Plan*

Chapter twenty-one

Divan Bed

Making a base for a divan bed is a fairly simple job. Softwood is generally used for the frame in present-day practice, although beech or birch were often used in less expensive days. Standard width sizes are ·75m., ·9m., 1·05m., 1·2m. and 1·350m. (2ft. 6in., 3ft., 3ft. 6in., 4ft. and 4ft. 6in.). Occasionally a 1·5m. (5ft.) width is required. 1·825 or 1·850m. (6ft. 2in. or 6ft. 3in.) is an average length: Extra tall people may wish to extend this to 1·950m. (6ft. 6in.) or even 2m. (6ft. 9in.). The depth of the side and end rails can be varied from 125 to 250mm. (5in. to 10in.) or more, according to the depth of springing required or a luxury appearance.

Many bases are made up with deep sides but the springing rails are set high up on the sides so only a 125mm. (5in.) spring is used. The frame in the design shown has four dumpy round screw-in legs, set on the end spring rails. Cut the side rails 1·850m. by 150mm. by 22mm. (6ft. 3in. by 6in. by $\frac{7}{8}$in.) planed finish. Join up to the required width of the end rails. The headboard end of the frame can be glued and screwed together or dovetailed and glued. The foot end looks neater if rounded, and is effected by fitting two shaped and notched blocks. This is shown in Fig. 2.

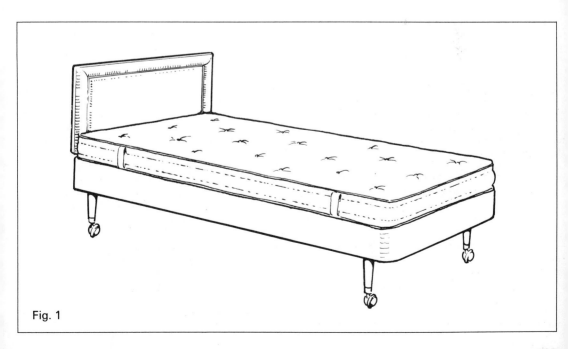

Fig. 1

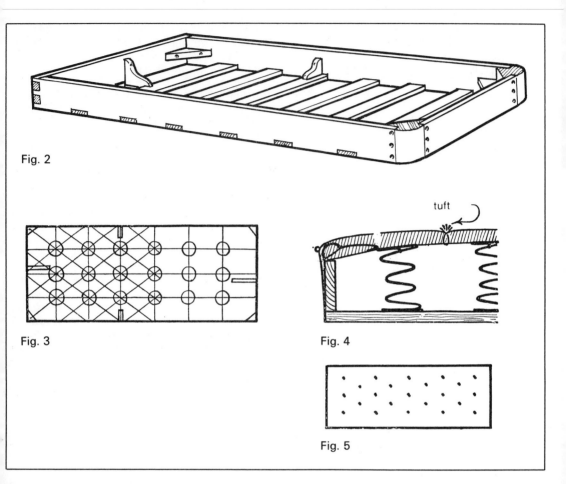

Fig. 2

Fig. 3

tuft

Fig. 4

Fig. 5

Six laths are needed for the springs spaced 175mm. (7in.) apart, excepting the two end ones which are spaced 200mm. (8in.) from the outside of the frame. Use 100mm. by 22mm. (4in. by $\frac{7}{8}$in.) timber and cut out the side rails to receive them. Glue and screw in position. Brackets should be fitted at the centre of each end rail, also at the centre of the side rails. A tie bracket fitted at each corner helps to make the frame rigid.

The legs are fixed on the undersides of the end springing rails at each corner on the single bed sides but six legs are safer on the double-bed sizes, especially if made to fold. Good castors should be fitted to the legs as beds have to be moved and under-sized castors only cause frayed tempers and worn carpets.

Springing First tack a 100mm. (4in.) wide strip of hessian across each rail to prevent the springs from making a noise. Three 7in. by 9- or 10-gauge springs to each rail, making eighteen in all, are required. Secure these to the framing by staples, three to each spring. The two side rows of springs are placed about 100mm. (4in.) from the inside of the frame. These are laced or lashed into position with laid cord or other strong, non-stretching cord.

Start lacing from side to side, first knocking a staple partly home opposite the centre of each row of springs. Thread an end of cord through these staples along one side, making each fast with a tie, then driving the staples home. Staples hold better than tacks for this job and do not split the deal so much.

110

Bring the cord to the top rung of the first spring and either knot or make a hitch round the wire. Proceed across each row of springs in this way, keeping the centre springs perfectly upright. The side springs all round should incline slightly towards the outside edge of the frame. After lacing crosswise proceed with lengthwise lacing, using the same method. Where the cords pass over each other take a single turn round the one already fixed. On a first-class job the springs would also be diagonally laced. This requires careful judgement to ensure the correct positioning of the springs, as all the lacing cords must be kept to an equal tension, Fig. 3.

Hessian When this has been completed proceed to hessian, using a stout quality, preferably the kind called tarpaulin. Fix it all round with temporary tacks first, then tack off the raw edge with $\frac{5}{8}$in. improved tacks. Leave about 18·75mm. ($\frac{3}{4}$in.) of spare hessian when trimming off, turning this over afterwards and tacking down. If the springs are diagonally laced it is not necessary to sew them to the hessian, otherwise sew in with three ties each, using a stout twine and spring needle. A small roll or edge all round is the next item, and this can either be of the tacked-on variety or a single-stitched type. To form the latter stitch a piece of scrim or cheap hessian on to the spring hessian. Turn under the raw edge and keep it parallel about 125mm. (5in.) from the edge of the frame. Stitch down with a half-circular needle and thin twine, making fairly long running stitches.

Stuffing Pick sufficient fibre under the scrim to bring the edge level with top of the centre springs. Do this all round, fixing with temporary tacks, until a firm, even edge is obtained, then tacking down. Tack with $\frac{1}{2}$in. improved tacks along a line about 25mm. (1in.) down on the outside of the frame. Regulate the stuffing well forward with a regulator or stout needle and make a single stitch all round. Start from the left-hand end, pushing the needle through close to the frame, taking up about 37·5mm. (1$\frac{1}{2}$in.) of scrim on top before returning and making a slip-knot. Pull tight and carry the needle along 75mm. (3in.) before inserting again. Return the needle about 37·5mm. (1$\frac{1}{2}$in.) behind its point of entry and this time make a single twist around the needle as it comes through. Carry on round the frame in this manner, pulling the twine tight to form an even edge.

Cover When this operation has been completed it is advisable to cut and fit the cover. Mattress ticking is the usual covering, but latterly other materials have been used with various results. Ticking is approximately 58in. wide, and 3 yards will be required. Cut the top piece 1·9m. by ·8m. (6ft. 4in. by 2ft. 8in.) thus allowing for the top stuffing and for stitching. Lay this piece on the job and shape the corners, not forgetting the allowances.

Next cut the border pieces about 225mm. (9in.) deep, three pieces being required. One width halved for each end and one width with a piece joined to each end for the side borders. Cut from the waste of the top for these joining portions. The borders are joined to the centre piece with a piped edge between. Make this up with odd pieces of tick cut on the cross about 31·25mm. (1$\frac{1}{4}$in.) wide. The top and sides are now machined together forming a piped, boxed border all round.

Top stuffing A thin top stuffing all over is the next item. Hair or fibre covered with a layer of linter's felt or a felted flock are all suitable. Run a few loops of twine round the edges about 50mm. (2in.) in, and pick a thin, even amount of stuffing under these. Lightly fill in the centre with an even layer of stuffing so that the tops of the springs can almost be felt, and cover with linter's felt, placing the cover over all, and easing down gently until the borders are in position. Temporarily tack all round then pull down further and tack again until the piped edge is level with the stitched edge.

The top is next marked out for tufting. Wool tufts give the nicest finish but cotton tufts or upholstery buttons can be used. Push a straight mattress needle through the tick to the spring hessian, catching about 18·75mm. ($\frac{3}{4}$in.) of the latter before returning. Tie a slip-knot on top and cut the twine, leaving about 150mm. (6in.) beyond the knot. Proceed to all the tufting points similarly before pushing the tufts under the slip-knots. Pull the knots tight and secure by knotting the twine before cutting off. Fig. 5 shows the position of the tufts.

The divan can now be turned on edge and the cover tacked down on the underside with $\frac{1}{2}$in. fine tacks. Finish off with a hessian bottom, turning under the raw edges and tacking off evenly.

The method described above is the older, traditional way of working and makes a first class, durable job. A more modern and easier way is to use the webbing over the springs, then cover with a fibre or hessian pad, tacking this down on the top of the rails all round. Cover the pad with a thick layer of linter's felt and the top is ready for the cover, as previously described.

Headboard The headboard can be almost any design to blend with existing furnishings. Either a polished wood or an upholstered wood type. illustrated on the sketch is a simple covered wood one. A piece of block board, particle board, or plywood covered with P.V.C. coated fabric makes quite a good finish. Mark out the border in pencil on the wood as at Fig. 6A, keeping the size in proportion to the height of the board desired. Cut a piece of 25mm. (1in.) low density poly-foam the size of the bottom panel. Fix this in position with a few dabs of adhesive and cover tautly with a piece of P.V.C.-coated fabric, tacked around the pencilled lines, and at the bottom pull under and tack off on the back. Measure the width and depth, plus tacking and sewing allowances of the border, which will be in three pieces. Temporarily tack the three pieces in position and cut the mitres on the top corners. Cut these tight so they will have to be pulled taut when tacking down. Machine sew the mitres together and make up a piece of piping to be sewn round the inside edge of the border. This completed, fix the border in position around the tacking line of the bottom panel, laying the border back on to this panel so it can be back-tacked along the piping as at C. Back-tack through a $\frac{1}{2}$in. strip of cardboard to give a clean finish. The back-tacking completed, cut strips of foam to fit the border spaces and stick this in position with adhesive D. Pull the border up and over the foam to temporary tack on the back of the headboard. Clean out the cover and make sure the foam is in place and even along the piping edge in particular. When satisfied you have a clean, taut finish tack off on the outside back. Complete the headboard by covering the outside back with the P.V.C. Fix the two supports or uprights in position by screwing them into place on the back of the board approximately 150mm. (6in.) inwards from the edges. Two headboard brackets should be screwed on to the divan base to engage the uprights.

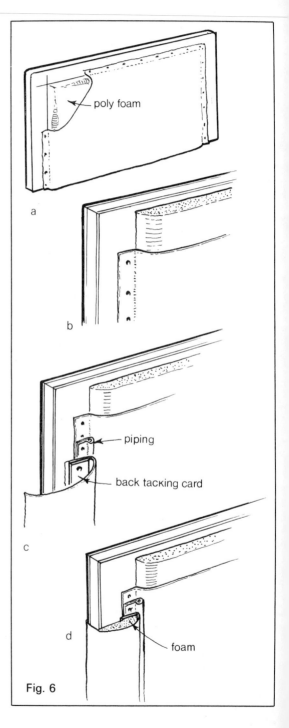

a

b

poly foam

piping

back tacking card

c

d

foam

Fig. 6

Chapter twenty-two

Deep Buttoned Headboard

The older head-and-foot type of bedstead has been largely replaced by the divan bed, and deep-buttoned headboards have become popular. The design illustrated is in traditional style and can be used in many decorative schemes. The framed method of construction is shown in Fig. 2. It is in 25mm. (1in.) planed softwood, cut to shape after being assembled with halved joints glued and screwed together.

A piece of stout hessian is tacked on all round, and pulled as taut as possible. A light hessian or scrim is tacked or sewn with twine around the edges of the frame. Under this hessian sufficient fibre is filled in to form a rill about 37·5mm. (1½in.) deep all round the edges and across the bottom approximately 175mm. (7in.) from the bottom rail. It is tacked down along the top edge of the shaped sides of the frame. A sink or blind stitch made with a twine and a mattress needle will bring the fibre forward to make a firmer edge all round.

Marking out The next item is to mark out on the hessian and frame the position of the buttons. Pencil a mark through the centre of the frame from top to bottom. Set out the lines for the buttons starting with one button at 75mm. (3in.) down from the

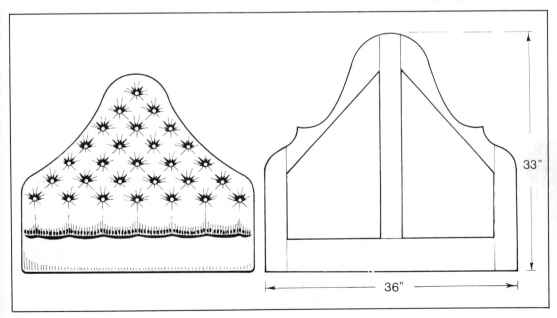

Fig. 1

Fig. 2 Framed construction.

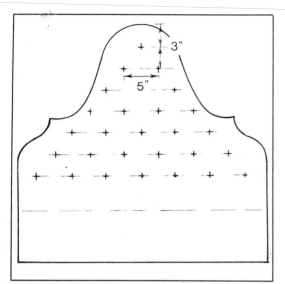

Fig. 3 Marking out for the buttons.
150mm. (6in.) by 125mm. (5in.) finished size;
187·5mm. (7½in.) by 162·5mm. (6½in.) cover
size.

top, and continue with parallel lines 75mm.
(3in.) apart until there are six lines below the first
button. On the first line make two marks 125mm.
(5in.) apart, that is 62·5mm. (2½in.) each side of
the centre line. On the next line make three marks,
and continue with the marking out to form diamond
spacing at 150mm. by 125mm. (6in. by 5in.). This
is about average for this size and type of headboard.

By using the latest material, such as blockboard,
chipboard, or ply, the frame can be cut out of one
piece and in this case no hessian is required. Mark
out the same sizes on one side of the board and
bore about 3·125mm. (⅛in.) hole at each button
mark to take needle and twine.

To obtain a deep buttoned finish with a polyether
foam filling a 2in. thick block of foam is required.
Cut this to the shape of the board allowing it to
overhang a trifle, as it will push back when the
cover is worked into position. A few dabs of
adhesive on both board and foam will help to keep
the latter in position whilst the buttons are tied
in. Pierce the foam at each button mark and make
a small hole so that the buttons can sink in.

The cover has also to be marked out for the buttons.
Covers vary as to the amount of fullness required to
obtain neat pleating! Approximately 37·5mm.
(1½in.) each way should be about right for the
traditional filling. If using 50mm. (2in.) foam on a
firm base 31·25mm. (1¼in.) would be about the
right amount to allow the pleats to set neatly and
cleanly. Commence the buttoning from the centre,
inserting the needle from the back and pushing it
through the filling to the corresponding cover
marking, taking the needle through the cover and
the back of the button. Return the needle through
the same hole in both cover and back board. Tie
the twine off with a slip-knot, and if on a solid
back, twist around a temporary tack. On a hessianed back insert a 25mm. (1in.) long roll of
waste material under the knot and pull fairly tight.
Cut the twine off six or seven inches below the
knot, and proceed with the remaining buttons in a
similar manner.

When they are loosely pulled down in place pass
around them and set the pleats, neatly folded
button to button, and all pulled down a little
tighter. Continue easing the cover over the sides
and bottom fixing with temporary tacks whilst
setting the pleats and cleaning out the fullness in
the process. When all the pleats are neatly set,
tack off on the edge and across the bottom.

Finally pull each button down tightly so all are
even, and finish with a knot on the twine above the
slip-knot. Cut off the twines above the knots on
the hessian back. On a wood back finish off the
same but wind the spare twine around the
temporary tack two or three times before driving
the tack home and cutting off the twine. Cut a
wide border to back-tack or sew across the bottom
of the headboard approximately 175mm. (7in.)
from the bottom edge. This is where the spring
interior mattress will fit into.

Make up a narrow border about 75mm. (3in.)
wide with a piping all along the top edge. This
border is to be tacked round the edge of the frame
to cover the tacking off of the front cover. Cut
some 12·5mm. (½in.) strips of cardboard to use for
back-tacking this border in position where the
piping lies just on the front edge of the wood
framing. Lay a narrow piece of linter's felt under
the border and tack off the border on the back of
the frame.

Fig. 4

Finish off the covering with a piece of matching lining on the outside back gimp pinned all round. A half thickness of linter's felt laid on the back before the lining will cover the feel of the knots etc.

Finally the headboard must be fixed to the divan base. Most bases have either bolts or brackets already fixed on their back end rails. Fix a pair of wood uprights in line with these fittings by screwing them to the back of the headboard with about three screws each.

An alternative design of a deep-buttoned headboard is given in Fig. 4. The general procedure is already given, but it is also helpful to read notes on the headboard in Chapter 21.

Chapter twenty-three

Deep Buttoning

It often happens that fashion turns a full cycle in the course of years. Furniture, and particularly upholstery, is no exception, and deep buttoned work, which is much in vogue at the present time, is a good example. It is a revival from the Victorian and Edwardian eras, when the older types of stuffing were in general use. Horsehair, fibre and flock were used in large quantities, these were 'loose' fillings worked on to the chair or settee by picking them under loops of twine to keep them in place. When thick layers of stuffing were being used, especially on curved surfaces, the loops were not always able to keep the stuffing in place. Hence the idea of buttoning was conceived and became popular for many years.

The job in hand was sprung and stuffed up to the first or scrim stuffing. Diamond formation was the usual pattern for deep buttoning, and this meant marking out the position and size of the diamonds. In some cases the marking out was carried out on the back of the job; in others it was done on the front. On a buttoned headboard the marking out is often done on the back; likewise on an unsprung chair or settee back. Sprung surfaces, where a first scrim stuffing is built up over the springs, are generally marked out on the top surface.

As an example, take the case of a spring-seated Victorian or Edwardian dining chair, the seat buttoned with ten buttons. The latter would be marked out on the scrim over a first stuffing of fibre and hair. Commence marking out by striking a crayon or blue pencil line across the centre of the seat from back to front. Cross this line at 87·5mm. to 100mm. (3½ to 4in.) from the front edge of the seat with the pencil, and again at 143·75mm. or 150mm. (5¾ or 6in.) from the first cross according to the size of the seat. There would be ten buttons used on an average chair of this type, and from the centre line it is simple to continue the marking out of the diamonds. The buttons would be placed at 143·75mm. or 150mm. by 175mm. (5¾ or 6in. by 7in.) giving three half diamonds. There are three buttons at the front, then two, three again, and two again, marked with crosses. Make a snip with the scissors at each mark and push the finger in to make a hole. This completes the marking out on the chair.

Left: A spring-seated Victorian dining chair.

Cover marking The cover also has to be marked out and the secret of successful buttoning is to allow the correct amount of fullness on it. With a fairly flat surface like this seat 37·5mm. by 37·5mm. (1½in. by 1½in.) fullness each way will be about the right amount for most materials. That is, the diamonds or position of the buttons would be spaced 187·5mm. by 212mm. (7½in. by 8½in.) on the cover for a 150mm. by 175mm. (6in. by 7in.) diamond on the scrim. Mark out the fabric with tailor's chalk or crayon, making a centre line first, and working from it as on the scrim. At each button mark on the cover push the regulator or a bradawl through to make a small but permanent hole which can be seen on the front of the cover.

The top stuffing is picked on to the scrim under loops of twine. When using hair pick it on evenly and mould together as the handfuls are pushed under the twine loops. Cover the hair with a thick layer of linter's felt. Feel through the linter's felt to each hole already snicked in the scrim. Cut off a length of good quality twine, and thread it through a double-pointed mattress needle. Push the needle through the marked cover to the centre button mark. Take it through to the spring hessian, catching up about 12·5mm. (½in.) before returning it to the top and through the cover alongside the twine already there. Bring the needle out and thread it through a button. Make a slip-knot above the button and cut off the twine about 175mm. (7in.) above the knot. Slip a small cutting of hessian or fabric through the loop of twine under the spring hessian. Pull the slip-knot down so that the button rests lightly in the stuffing. Leave the button in that position for the time being, and proceed in a similar manner with the remainder of the buttons. When they are about level work round the outside edges and level off, working in the pleats cleanly, and temporarily tack down on the sides, back, and front of the frame. Repeat the pulling down of the slip-knots, at the same time cleaning out and forming the pleats all round. Release the temporary tacks at the sides and tack down more tightly and cleanly. When all the pleats are in position and folded down towards the front complete the tacking down all round. Give each twine a final pull down before making a knot on the twine as close as possible to the button shank above the slip-knot so that it cannot slip off or up. Cut off the twine near the knot. Take the flat end of the regulator and tuck the knotted twine under the button.

Curved surfaces The foregoing remarks have dealt with the traditional methods of buttoning a small and more or less flat seat. A concave back of a chair would probably need only 25mm. (1in.) in the width of the diamond by 37·5mm. (1½in.) depth. Rounded surfaces like the back of a chesterfield settee would need a lot more fullness. The marking out on the scrim would be the same except that it would be done in half diamonds over the back. Three rows is an average number, that is a diamond and a half. The marking out is started 87·5mm. to 100mm. (3½in. to 4in.) from the outer edge of the scrim stuffing on the top of the back. The next two rows at 3½in. apart and the bottom row at 3¾in. apart. The width of the diamonds depends on the length of the settee and build up of the scrolls. Around 131mm. to 150mm. (5¼in. to 6in.) is the average width. The holes are snipped in the same way and the top stuffing picked on as usual. It should be a good thick layer covered with linter felt.

Marking out the cover is rather different as it has to go over a big curve. On the first row upwards from the seat 18·75mm. (1in.) fullness will be enough for most fabrics on the length of the half diamond by 37·5mm. (1½in.) in width. This width allowance is continued on all rows, but the length fullness must be increased considerably over the curve of the back. In all an allowance of 112·5mm. (4½in.) should preferably be made; 62·5mm. (2½in.) over the main curve, the second half diamond, and 50mm. (2in.) on the last. Occasionally, 56·25mm. and 56·25mm. (2¼in. and 2¼in.) may be used according to the shaping of the first stuffing but the first arrangement seems to give a nice upright half diamond. Allow at least 62·5mm. (2½in.) on the pull over for tacking off. An inset piece of cover must be cut for both mitred bottom half diamonds, this being stitched in when the back and scrolls covers are joined together. Whenever dealing with button work be generous rather than mean with fullness. You can tuck away a little extra fullness but nothing looks worse than a strained diamond with the pleats pulling out.

Modern materials This brings us to buttoning over modern fillings, latex and poly-foams. The same marking out must be done but usually it is on the back of the hessian as no scrim stuffing is needed. Alternatively, the foam is marked out on top and small holes cut at each button mark so that

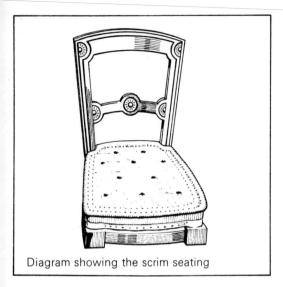

Diagram showing the scrim seating

the buttons sink in. One disadvantage with foam is that pleats and seams do not bed into it so well as on the older types of fillings. That is one reason why a large proportion of button work has the pleats machined in place, especially on hard covers such as the P.V.C. coated fabrics. It is often difficult to get these pleats to lie flat and keep in position without stitching. A generous fullness allowance with the pleats pressed in on the back when marking out will help.

Foams take a lot of the hard work out of the building up of upholstery and give clean finishes if properly used. The older loose fillings are still needed for many specialised jobs and antiques. Perhaps it is as well to remember the opening remarks that buttoning was a traditional method of upholstering, whereas the foams are the latest forms of fillings and should be treated as such.

Chapter twenty-four

Running Repairs

Fig. 1

Like most things in constant use, chairs and sette eventually need renovating. Many of them hav webbed and hand sprung seats; others hav. 'patent' sprung seats, single springs, and double-sprung units which have become crippled or lop-sided and uncomfortable. Provided the frames are in reasonable condition and free from woodworm it should be possible to renovate and recover most of the casualties. Some frames may have loose joints, and these need to be knocked apart, reglued and cramped back into position. Timber of most types has quite a long life and does not require a lot of expensive machinery to repair or alter its form.

The chair in Fig. 1 is one cf a three-piece suite of two easies and a three-seater settee with cushions. This suite is not in a bad condition as it is not very old. The cover has become worn and dirty in places so it was decided to recover it in a plain tweed fabric. Apart from the stuffing, fibre, lintafelt, and flattening on the arms and seats there was little wrong with the springing.

Commence the job by turning one of the easies up-side down, resting the seat on a stool or dining chair. Remove the hessian bottom by knocking out the tacks with the ripping chisel and mallet. Continue knocking out all the tacks holding the cover in place except for one or two holding tacks at the top of the inside back. Remove all outside covers and the two inside arms, but leave a couple of tacks at the bottom of the front border to keep the stuffing in place.

The tops of the arms have flattened and there is a hollow near the front. The stuffing consists of fibre both coco and black Algerian covered with lintafelt. Lift up the whole of the top stuffing and push some extra fibre under it to bring it all up to an even surface. If a piece of 12·5mm. or 18·75mm. ($\frac{1}{2}$in. or $\frac{3}{4}$in.) foam is laid over the top portion of the arm it will ensure an even finish. Cutting the cover is the next item. Some upholsterers would prefer to cut the covers from their own measurements. Others would take all sections of the old covers and use them as patterns to cut from. This is quite all right if they are a good fit and the stuffing is picked over and brought up to its original shape.

Seat platforms The chair in Fig. 1, has the tops of the arms cut to shape and piped. As this is a

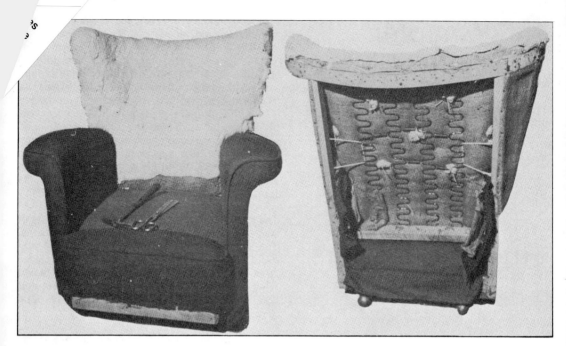

Fig. 2

Fig. 3

cushion seated chair the seat is made up of the front platform piece with a lining over the back portion, also called the platform. The front platform is cut about 6in. wide and fitted to shape on the top of the seat. Cut the top part of the border and join to the platform with a piping around the front edge. Join up a piece of matching lining to the edge of the platform. Also stitch a piece of binding tape, half a web or stout piece of old cover, along that joined up edge of the platform and lining.

Lay this across the seat in the original hollow, pushing the ends of the binding or web under the arms each side, fixing with a tack at each end on the seat rails. Using a half-circular needle and twine, sew through the binding and seam and catch the hessian over the springs thus, holding both cover and lining in the hollow.

Seat stuffing As the stuffing of the seat is flat and broken up, the fibre is picked over and opened out with some more added to it. A new piece of lintafelt is laid over both back and front portions. The lining is pushed over the stuffing and down between seat and back; also between the arms

down each side. Fix all round with temporary tacks. Bring the front platform and border to the front edge of the seat. Temporarily hold here with about three skewers pushed through the piping seam into the scrim stuffing. Pick over and even out the border stuffing, if it is not strung in run two or three loops of twine across and pick the fibre under it. Cover with a piece of linterfelt, then re-remove the skewers and pull the border over the stuffing to the front seat rail fixing it temporarily.

Attention can now be given to the arm covers which should be piped and sewn ready to be laid over the top of the foam on the arm. Try to avoid dislodging the foam or the stuffing as the cover is eased over and temporarily tacked all round. Clean out any creases or uneven stuffing. Pull the piping on the front facing down very taut to the bottom of the front facing and temporarily fix. Clean out along the top edge and on the arm tacking rail, using fixing tacks until all the cover is cut and clean. Start tacking off both arms all round, then the seat sides and back, finally the front border on the front of the seat main rail. This should be approximately 50mm. to 75mm. (2in.

Fig. 4

adding another piece if necessary. Push the bottom of the inside back cover through the opening between the seat and back and fix this bottom edge along the back tacking rail with about three temporary tacks. Pull the remaining cover up and over the inside back, fixing it with temporary tacks along the top back rail.

Smooth out the cover widthways and get a temporary tack on each wing side rail, also pushing the 'flys' on the piped cut outs on the back through between the arms and back. With the cover roughly fixed in position start to strain and clean out all round, ready for tacking off.

Buttoning Before doing so, fix the buttons in place. Mark out the positions with a small chalk mark. In this case, the top buttons are placed 250mm. (10in.) from the outer edge of the top back rail and 167·5mm. (6½in.) between widthways, 125mm. (5in.) between each row downwards. In this case of a repair job, follow the old markings on the hessian covering the springs. Some of the original ties are seen in Fig. 3. Use a double pointed needle and twine pushing it through from the back, picking up a button before returning to the back and tying with a slip-knot. Pull down the buttons fairly tightly, then finish tacking off the back cover all round. Now complete tying off the buttons, and start finishing off the lower, narrow front border and the outsides. These are all back-tacked on the top edges and pulled down and tacked off on the undersides of the seat rails.

The outside back and wings can be given a piped finish by making up a piece of piping to pass from wing to wing. It can be machined across the top of the wing and outside back and this portion back-tacked in place. The sides of the wings and outside arms are finished by slip-stitching or gimp pinned. Complete the chair with a new hessian or lining bottom. Cutting the cushion is a simple job, measure round the existing cushion meeting the tape in the centre of the back border. Also measure the width and cut the cover to these sizes plus sewing allowance. Pin the cover in place and cut borders to fit each side. Make nicks or chalk marks where they meet the front edge and the back. Remove the cover and machine same. Preferably inserting a piping around each side border. Once again the cushion covers can be closed, with zip fasteners or slip-stitching.

to 3in.) up from the bottom edge. A narrow finishing border is back-tacked across the front and a piece of linterfelt laid under it before tacking off on the underside of the front rail.

The back can now be attended to. Remove the old cover which has been left over the back stuffing so it was not displaced whilst working on the seat and arms. Note the position of the buttons and re-mark on the back hessian if necessary. Measure over the inside back and wings and cut to size. Lay this cover over the back and clean out and fix as far as possible. Where this cover meets the inside arms, clean it out as close as possible before making a cut near the top of the arm to get the cover closer to the arm. When this is achieved push the cover up as close as possible to the arm and mark round the back cover with chalk. Repeat at each arm and carefully cut to the shape plus the sewing allowance. Sew the piping around the cut out and add a 'fly', also sewn round to shape. This is to tuck in between the arms and back. Before starting to cover the back pick over the stuffing and add extra if needed. Replace the lintafelt,

Cushions The cushions on this suite are foamed rubber and in a fair condition although a little skimped in depth. A piece of 25mm. (1in.) foam is added to each unit and stuck in place with rubber adhesive. After long use latex cushions perish and start to crumble or break up in places. Polyether foam cushions compress and flatten especially on the front edges. When either has happened it is advisable to replace with new units. The settee, a three seater, is dealt with in a similar manner to the chairs. Three cushions will be needed on the seat and the inside back will be piped in two places to avoid unsightly joins in a plain cover. 15·3m. (17yds.) of plain fabric were required and 1·8m. (2yds.) of lining for the seat platforms.

Loose seats A loose seat, as its name implies, is made on a frame separate or loose from the main frame, and is used on many different types of chairs and stools.

Stripping the old materials Remove the seat from the chair and place it upside-down on a bench or table. Start to take off the bottom hessian (if any) and the cover by removing the tacks holding these materials in place, using a ripping chisel and mallet, as in Fig. 5. An old screwdriver can be used as a substitute for the ripping chisel. Drive out the tacks *with* the grain of the wood whenever possible so as to avoid splitting if the seat is cramped to the bench with a G cramp it makes the work easier. Having cleared the tacks on the bottom of the frame turn it over and remove the cover and stuffing. The hessian and webs can then be stripped off in the same way.

Quite often it will be found that plywood has been used as a base for the stuffing. This should be examined to see that it is sound. If it has split it should be discarded, otherwise it may cause squeaking when the chair is used. The nails holding it should be tight, and if necessary fresh nails should be driven in. Glue and cramp any loose joints.

Webbing The ripping completed, the remaking of the seat is started by fixing fresh webbing. The average size seat requires two strands of web each way, though some larger chairs need three webs. The wide, early Victorian type of chair or a long narrow stool needs a different arrangement—two by three or two by four strands are often necessary.

Fig. 5 Knocking off or removing the old cover. Note that the ripping chisel or old screwdriver is always worked in the direction of the grain so that any splitting tendency is avoided.

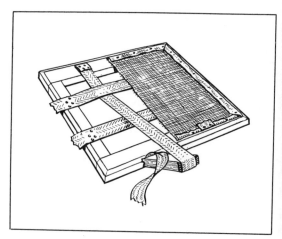

Fig. 6 Use of strainer when re-webbing. The hessian is tacked on after the webbing is finished. Note that the edges are double thus obviating any tendency for them to pull through.

Note the original spacing of the webbing when ripping, and follow the same plan.

The webs are tacked on from the back to the front and from left to right as a general rule. Tack on by turning over the web about 25mm. (1in.) and using ⅝in. improved tacks, spaced as shown in Fig. 6. Stretch to the opposite rail with a web strainer and tack down, leaving 25mm. (1in.) of web over when cutting off. This is turned over later with the hessian and held down with two tacks. Proceed with the other webs in a similar manner, checking the side ones under and over alternatively before straining.

A piece of hessian is tacked over the webs, starting from the back rail. Turn over the hessian and tack on with ½in. or ⅜in. improved tacks. Pull as tight as possible to the front rail and tack down through one thickness of hessian, leaving about 18·75mm. (¾in.) for turning. Repeat this operation from side to side, and finally double over the turnings and the webbing ends.

The stuffing on a webbed seat may be broken up and uneven, and will need carding, that is, broken up or pulled apart by a carding machine. The latter are becoming scarce with the passing of loose fillings. Unless the seat comes from a chair which is a valuable antique it will probably be advisable to put a thin layer of hair, fibre, or flock on the hessian and cover it with a 25mm. (1in.) thick piece of foam cut to shape. This makes quite a good seat. If a firmer seat is required more of the old stuffing should be used and a thinner piece of foam.

Many loose seats are covered with P.V.C. fabrics and occasionally hide. If these are being used it is often easier to cover the stuffed seat with calico first. Lay the calico over the stuffing and fix in place with about three temporary tacks on each side. Gradually ease down all round and tack off evenly on the outer edge of the frame. Keep the filling clear of the outer edge so that it is clean all round. Use ⅜in. fine tacks and drive them well home. Aim at a nicely rounded contour, rather more to the front than to the centre of the seat.

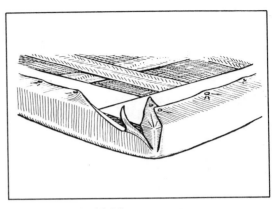

Fig. 7 Method of folding cover at corner. The centre is taken straight across and is tacked. A fold is then made at each side. ·

Complete the covering with the chosen material, following the same methods as with the calico, except that this time the fabric is tacked off on the bottom edge of the frame, not on the side edge. If P.V.C. material is being used it will probably require several fixings before finally tacking down. The fullness or surplus caused by the rounded shape of the seat needs pulling and easing down until the top is clean and clear of all rucks or folds. A tapestry or soft cover is easier to work into place as there is more stretch or give.

When satisfied that the top is clean finally tack off on the underside with ⅜in. or ½in. fine tacks. Start at the sides, then the front and back, leaving the corners until last. Usually the best method with the corners is to pull the centre of the spare material over the actual point of the corner and make a fold on each side of this point with the remaining surplus material as in Fig. 7. Keep the folds or pleats as tight and small as possible. A piece of hessian neatly turned under at the edges and tacked on to hide the tacks and raw edges of the cover makes a clean finish. This bottom, as it is called, is not a necessity, but finishes the job neatly. Many seats are finished without bottoms, the rough edges and surplus cover being trimmed off neatly with a knife.

Index

Air tools, 12
Algerian fibre, 14
Alva, 13
Armchair, wing, 75

Bead moulding, 44
Black flock, 13, 34
Box ottoman, 105–108
  slipper, 50, 54
Buttoned stool, 53
Buttoning, deep, 116–119
  headboard, 114

Cabriole hammer, 9
Calico, 15, 24, 33, 34, 47
Casement cloth, 37
Castors, 78
Chesterfield frame, 30
Chisel, ripping, 10
Coco fibre, 14, 83
Cord, various, 15
Corner pleat, 35, 48
Cover for loose seat, 48
Covers, measuring, 38, 39
  planning and cutting,
    36–40, 69, 72, 76, 77,
    88, 89, 96, 99, 103, 119
Cowhide leathers, 42
Cushions, feather, 39
  latex, 15, 39, 59, 70, 77, 90

Divan bed, 109
Double spring unit, 22
Dressing-table stool, 52

Eiderdown feathers, 14

Feather cushions, 24

Fibreglass, 29, 72
Fibres, 34
Filling materials, 34
Flexibead, 44
Flock, 14
Flys, 37, 89
Frames, box ottoman, 105
  chair, 27–31
  cushioned three-piece suite,
    101, 102
  divan bed, 109
  fireside easy, 56, 60, 63
  modern three-piece suite,
    78
  seat, 45
  sizes, 28
  stools, 52, 53
  television or sewing chair,
    67
  three-piece suite, 78
  wing chair, 75

Gimp, 51, 52
Ginger fibre, 14, 83

Hair, horse, 13, 14, 34, 47
Hammers, 9
Headboard, 112, 113–115
Hessian, 13, 15, 33, 37, 47,
  50
Hides, 33, 37, 38, 41–44, 45,
48
  buffed, 42
  fullgrain, 42

Horsehair, 13, 14, 34, 47

Iron back chair, 27

Kapok, 13, 14

Laid cord, 15
Latex, foamed, 11, 12, 15, 16, 62, 70, 77, 90, 102
Leathercloth, 33, 45
Linsey wool, 13
Lintafelt, 11, 12, 14
Linter's felt, 34, 46, 76
Loose seats, 45

Material for covers, 36
    joining, 36
    patterned, 36
Moquette, 36
Moroccos, 41–44

Needles, 11
No-sag springs, 26

Open arm fireside chair, 60
Ottoman, box, 105–108

Patent springing, 20
Pincushion seats, 49
Piping, 37, 38, 40, 51
    cord, 15
Pleat, corner, 35, 48
Polyether, 11, 12
Polyurethane foam, 29
Power tools, 12
Pullover, 70
PVC fabrics, 10, 34, 37, 38, 42, 48

Rasp, 11
Repairs, upholstery, 119–123
Ripping chisel, 10, 11

Roans, 41, 42
Roll or edge stitching, 35
Rolls, facings, etc., 44, 50
Rubber webbing, 17, 26, 62, 64
Ruchings, 38

Scissors, 9, 10
Scrim, 13, 33, 34
    stuffing, 13
Seams, 38
Seats, loose, 45
    pincushion, 49
Serpentine springs, 25
Settee frames, 29
Sewing machine, 12
Shell frames, 29, 72
Single spring unit, 20
Skewer, 11
Skiving, 42
Slip-knot, 33
Slipper box, 50, 54
Spring, canvas, 13
    units, 20–22
Springing, 20–26
    back of fireside chair, 57
Springs, coil, 78, 110
    tension, 20, 23, 25, 77, 95
    zig-zag, 26
Staples, 9
Stapling gun, 9, 12
Stool covers, 51
    dressing-table, 46
    frame joints, 51
Stools, various, 50–55
Strainers, web, 10, 47
Studs, 15
Suite, cushioned three-piece,

101–104
    modern three-piece, 93–100
    three-piece, 78–92
Swivel chair, 74

Tack hammer, 9
Tacking, method of, 32
Tacks, 9, 15
Tarpaulin (hessian), 13, 111
Tension springs, 20, 23, 25, 77, 95
Tools, 9
Trestle work, 11, 12
Tub easy chair, 28
Twine work, 33
Twines, 15

Units, spring–single, double, triple, 20–26
Upholder's Company, 7
Upholstery, early history, 7
    repairs, 119–123

Vegetable fibres, 14
Velcro fastening, 31
Velvet, 36

Wadding, 15, 34
Web pincers, 10, 11
    strainers, 10, 47
Webbing, 13, 15, 32, 46, 50, 60, 75, 78
Wing armchair, 75
    settee frame, 30
Wood facings, 38, 44

Zig-zag springing, 26